CB081715

MICKEY ROGERS
JOANNE TAYLORE-KNOWLES
STEVE TAYLORE-KNOWLES

SPEAK YOUR MIND

STUDENT'S BOOK
+ access to Student's App and Digital Workbook

3B

macmillan education

	Outcomes	Vocabulary	Grammar	Speaking
Unit 7 Looking Back pp. 67–75	• Talk about things that a business should have done differently • Discuss things you should not have bought • Recall events you regret	• Phrasal verbs • *spend, lose, waste* • Collocations	• *Should/shouldn't have* • Past perfect for wishes about the past Grammar Reference pp 151–152	• Talk about what people should have done differently • Talk about things you regret buying • Tell an anecdote
	Language and Life—Interpersonal Communication: Plan and Give a Presentation about a Product			
Unit 8 A New Home? pp. 77–85	• Talk about hypothetical events in history • Role play an interview with an astronaut • Discuss your opinions of space exploration	• Extinction of the dinosaurs • Space • Space program inventions	• Third conditional • Indirect questions Grammar Reference pp 152–153	• Speculate about alternative histories • Role-play an interview • Discuss space exploration
	Language and Life—Reason Effectively: Select a Space Team			
Unit 9 The World of News pp. 87–95	• Give your opinions on fake news, journalists and citizen journalists • Compare real and fake news stories • Role-play a job interview for a news career	• News • News stories • News careers	• *So, such, too, enough* • Modals of deduction Grammar Reference pp 154–155	• Discuss news now • Discuss how you knew a news story was true or fake • Role-play a job interview
	Language and Life—Problem Solving: Discuss Ideas to Improve Newspaper Sales			
Unit 10 Got It? pp. 97–105	• Talk about your talents and abilities • Ask and answer questions for a talent show audition • Share advice on how to succeed in the music industry	• Talents and abilities • Phrasal verbs • Idioms and sayings connected to success	• Reported speech: statements • Reported speech: questions Grammar Reference pp 155–156	• Talk about something someone can do well • Talk about talent show contestants • Discuss the usefulness of advice
	Language and Life—Communication: Hold a Talent Contest			
Unit 11 Money in the Bank pp. 107–116	• Discuss who you would employ if you were a millionaire • Share ideas about what to do with a fortune • Compare your budget with that of a partner	• Money • Money verbs and nouns • Paying for things	• Causatives with *have, get* and *make* • Verbs with gerund, infinitive or both Grammar Reference pp 156–158	• Discuss jobs to do yourself • Talk about how to use a lot of money • Talk about monthly budgets
	Language and Life—Collaborate: Manage a Budget			
Unit 12 Inside Advertising pp. 117–126	• Discuss the advertising of energy drinks • Talk about ads that you like and dislike • Debate the effects of advertising	• From the reading Advertising • Advertising campaigns • Discourse markers	• Passive voice: other tenses • Comparative and superlative adverbs Grammar Reference pp 158–159	• Discuss whether to ban advertisements • Talk about improving ad campaigns • Debate the effects of images in advertising
	Language and Life—Media Literacy: Make a TV Ad			

Confident Communicator	Pronunciation	Listening/Reading	Thinking Skills	Writing
Start Talking • Tell an anecdote *Keep Talking* • Give reasons *Start Talking* • Set the scene	• /s/ and /z/	Read an online article about famous mistakes • Skill—Synthesize Listen to a radio interview about regret • Skill—Listen for reasons Listen to a talk about types of regret • Skill—Listen for main ideas	• Evaluate • Analyze • Apply	Write a blog post about regrets
Unit Review p. 76 **Study Skills**—Structuring Your Writing				
Keep Talking • Express probability *Keep Talking* • Ask polite questions *Keep Talking* • Clarify reasons for opinions	• Consonant clusters with /s/	Read an article about the dinosaurs • Skill—Predict Listen to an interview about life in space • Skill—Listen for specific information Listen to a panel discussion about space • Skill—Listen for main ideas	• Analyze • Question • Recall	Write a blog post about space exploration
Unit Review p. 86 **Follow a Pro**—An Astrobiologist ▶ Astronomer				
Keep Talking • Ask for opinions *Repair It* • Interrupt politely *Keep Talking* • Interview techniques	• /ə/ versus /r/	Read texts about news • Skill—Identifying text types Listen to a lecture about fake news • Skill—Listen for information order Listen to an interview about being a foreign correspondent • Skill—Listen for opinions	• Analyze • Apply • Deduce	Write about a job
Unit Review p. 96 **Study Skills**—Making Notes				
Keep Talking • Your achievements *Keep Talking* • Talk in front of a group *Keep Talking* • Use idioms carefully	• Stress in phrasal verbs	Read a text about great artists • Skill—Recognize fact and opinion Listen to excerpts from a TV talent show • Skill—Identify attitude Listen to a radio call-in show about the music industry • Skill—Listen to take notes	• Question • Analyze • Evaluate	Write an informal email
Unit Review p. 106 **Follow a Pro**—A Talent Scout ▶ Musician				
Start Talking • Talk about imagined future situations *Start Talking* • Collaborate on creative ideas *Keep Talking* • Talk or avoid talking about money	• /tʃ/ versus /ʃ/	Read a job ad, article and business profile about the gig economy • Skill—Read for the main idea Listen to an interview about charity • Skill—Listen for specific information Listen to a radio show about managing money • Skill—Listen for the main idea	• Question • Apply • Recall	Write an email listing key points
Unit Review p. 116 **Study Skills**—Personal Development				
Keep Talking • Take turns in a discussion *Repair It* • Getting back on track *Keep Talking* • Paraphrase	• Filler sounds and words	Read an article about advertising • Skill—Identify missing sentences Listen to an ad • Skill—Listen for inference Listen to an interview about advertising • Skill—Recognize discourse markers	• Evaluate • Symbolize • Induce	Write a 'for' and 'against' essay about retouching images
Unit Review p. 126 **Follow a Pro**—A Digital Copywriter ▶ Video Editor				

Grammar Quiz: What Do You Already Know?

A Complete the paragraph with the simple past, past progressive, or present perfect form of the verbs in parentheses.

Colombian teen Yadis Xiomara Chocó Mina has a clear goal: to help others. She **1** _____________ (work) to improve the lives of young girls since she was nine years old. She **2** _____________ (work) with a group called Plan International Colombia when she first **3** _____________ (start) to mentor young girls in her community. Since then, she **4** _____________ (not stop). A few years ago, while she **5** _____________ (visit) Spain, she **6** _____________ (become) mayor of Madrid for a day as part of International Day of the Girl. Yadis has big plans: someday she wants to be Colombia's minister of education.

B Complete the email message with the correct quantifiers from the box.

a few   a little   a lot of   any   enough   too much

New Message

Hi Anna,

I'm home preparing for Ricardo's graduation party. I've finished most of the preparations, but I could use **1** _____________ help. There are going to be **2** _____________ people here—I think about 45 of his friends are coming. We have 40 chairs, but it's not **3** _____________. Can you bring **4** _____________ chairs—maybe three or four? I know we have **5** _____________ food, so there will be leftovers for the guests to take home. So, please don't bring **6** _____________ more food. There is nowhere to put it!

See you soon,
Bev

C Choose the correct option.

1 Can / Would you like to join us?
2 I'm sure Oscar will / may be here.
3 Will / May I put my jacket here?
4 Could / May you please take a seat?
5 Lena might / would be late for the wedding.
6 They probably won't / might not be there.

D Complete the sentences with the correct form of the verb in parentheses.

1 If you _____________ (eat) a lot of sugar, you gain weight.
2 If I _____________ (have) more time, I would exercise more.
3 You will enjoy these brain puzzles if you _____________ (try) them.
4 If I _____________ (get) tired at the library, I usually take a short nap.
5 I probably _____________ (not go) to the hospital if I had a bad cold.
6 You _____________ (not feel) better if you don't take this medicine.

E Find one error in each sentence. Then rewrite the sentences correctly.

1 Maggie has belonged to a gym since 15 years.

____

2 Rafael hasn't graduated from high school already.

____

3 A lot cans and plastic are recycled these days.

____

4 People use to buy a lot of music CDs in the 1990s.

____

5 Jae is the more adventurous person in my family.

____

6 Students need to introduce themself in class.

____

Go to the Grammar Review on pages 140–141.

UNIT 7

Looking Back

WHAT DO YOU ALREADY KNOW?

1 Think of words about things people sometimes regret. Write the words.

2 **IN PAIRS** Share and compare your ideas. Add more words to your lists.

Regrets

VIDEO

DISCUSS & SHARE

3 **IN GROUPS** Watch the video and answer the question.

SYM Do you think it's good to have regrets, or is it better to focus on the future?

In this unit, you will ...

- talk about things that a business should have done differently, discuss things you should not have bought, and recall events you regret.
- use thinking skills: evaluate, analyze, and apply.
- read about famous mistakes in history.
- use strategies and language to introduce an anecdote, give reasons for opinions and decisions, and set the scene for a story.
- use interpersonal communication skills to plan and give a presentation.
- learn skills to structure your writing.

Famous Mistakes

READING

A **IN GROUPS THINKING SKILL—Evaluate** **Assess a description of the "butterfly effect." Do you think the statement is true, partly true, or false? Explain.**

A butterfly moves its wings in Brazil, and it creates a storm in Texas.

B 7.01 **Read the article about famous mistakes. Is either of the mistakes an example of the butterfly effect?**

Famous Mistakes in History

1. Expensive Decision

In the 1982 mega-hit movie *E.T.* there is a scene where the little boy uses candy to convince *E.T.* the extraterrestrial, to follow him. The filmmakers had planned to use M&Ms for this scene, but Mars, Inc. did not give them permission to use their candy. They then asked Hershey for permission to use Reese's Pieces, and Hershey agreed, so it **turned out** that Reese's Pieces candy was used in the movie. Two weeks after the movie opened, sales of Reese's Pieces **went up** by around 65%. Today, a Reese's product is the number one candy in the US! Mars Inc. shouldn't have missed this opportunity!

2. Lost in Space

The Mars Climate Orbiter was a small spacecraft built to orbit Mars and record information about the surface and atmosphere of the planet. It went into space in December 1998, and it disappeared in September 1999. When researchers **looked into** why the Orbiter was lost, they **came across** an important mistake. They **found out** that the system on the spacecraft had used the metric system, while the computers on Earth had used the imperial system. Because of this mistake, the Orbiter went too close to Mars and **burned up**. Someone should have noticed that the two systems used different measurements!

GLOSSARY

metric system (n): a system of measurement that uses meters and kilograms
imperial system (n): a system of measurement that uses yards and pounds
orbit (v): the path of an object moving around a larger object in space
measurement (n): the exact size of something, expressed in numbers of standard units

C **READING SKILL—Synthesize** **Match the descriptions below to the famous mistakes in B. Write the numbers.**

1 a mistake caused by different people using different systems _____
2 a mistake that was very lucky for a competitor _____

VOCABULARY phrasal verbs

A **Match the phrasal verbs in bold in READING B to the definitions (1–6). Write the base form of each phrasal verb.**

1 ________________ : to investigate an event or situation
2 ________________ : to have a certain result
3 ________________ : to discover information
4 ________________ : to meet someone or discover something by chance
5 ________________ : to be destroyed by fire or heat
6 ________________ : to increase

B **Choose the correct phrasal verbs.**

When companies have poor sales, they have to **1** come across / look into the reasons why a product doesn't sell. When they do research, they sometimes **2** find out / turn out that the problem is with the marketing, but sometimes it **3** finds out / turns out that the problem is the product itself. The company may have to stop developing that product and develop a new product. This is not always a problem. Sometimes a series of mistakes can result in new products that make the company's sales **4** look into / go up a lot.

GRAMMAR *should/shouldn't have*

A **Choose the correct options.**

Someone should have noticed that the two systems used different measurements!
Mars Inc. shouldn't have missed this opportunity!

1 *Should have* and *shouldn't have* are used to express …
a recommendations for the past.
b recommendations for the present.
c recommendations for the future.

2 *Should have* and *shouldn't have* are followed by the … form of a verb.
a base form
b simple past
c past participle

For more practice, go to page 151.

B **Complete the responses using *should have* or *shouldn't have* and the correct form of the verb in parentheses.**

1 A British couple asked a lottery official to check their lottery ticket numbers. The official checked the numbers and told the couple that they had not won any money. The official tore the ticket in two pieces and threw it away. However, the couple later received a message to keep their ticket. They got the torn ticket from the lottery official, and it turned out that they had won 57.9 million euros!
The official *should have checked* (check) the numbers more carefully. / The official *shouldn't have thrown away* (throw away) the ticket.

2 In 1999, a company called Excite had the opportunity to buy Google. The heads of Google wanted one million dollars, but then they changed the price to $750,000. Excite thought it was too expensive and turned down the offer. Today, Google is worth billions of dollars.
Excite ________________ (buy) Google. / Excite ________________ (turn down) the offer.

3 J. K. Rowling's first book, *Harry Potter and the Philosopher's Stone*, was turned down by 12 publishers before it was published by Bloomsbury. One reason why Bloomsbury decided to publish the book was that the chief executive officer's eight-year-old daughter read part of the book and loved it.
The 12 publishers ________________ (turn down) the book. / The 12 publishers ________________ (accept) the book.

C **IN PAIRS Take turns reading the responses in B. Do you have similar opinions?**

SPEAKING

A **Think of a mistake that a person or a company made and consider what they should have done differently. Use the questions as a guide and make notes.**

1 Who was the person or what was the company?
2 What mistakes did the person or company make?
3 What should they have done differently?
4 How did the situation turn out?

B **IN GROUPS Tell your group what happened. Say what you think the person or company should have done differently. Discuss other possible options with your group. Use the Confident Communicator box to help you.**

CONFIDENT COMMUNICATOR
START TALKING

To introduce an anecdote or a short true story, use these phrases:
Here's something that happened to (person/company) in (date).
Listen to this. In (date), (name) made a really bad decision.

LESSON 2 Why Did I Buy That?

VOCABULARY *spend, lose, waste*

A Write *spend*, *lose*, or *waste*.

1 ______________ : to have less money because of mistake
2 ______________ : to use money or time to get something
3 ______________ : to use money or time in a careless way

B Choose the correct words.

1 Many people waste / lose a lot of money buying unnecessary things.
2 Making a financial plan can help you waste / spend your money carefully.
3 If you buy lottery tickets, you are probably just wasting / spending your money.
4 Many people lost / wasted a lot of money when stock prices fell.
5 My uncle started a small company, but it failed. He spent / lost all of his money.

LISTENING

A IN PAIRS Which of these things do you think people often regret buying? Discuss.

1 
vacation homes

2 
a desktop computer

3 
exercise equipment

4 
collectible objects

5 
a new car

6 
a swimming pool or a hot tub

B 7.02 Listen to the radio interviews. Check (✓) the items in A they discuss.

GLOSSARY

regret (v): to feel sorry or sad about something that happened
regret (n): a feeling of sadness about something that happened

MAKE IT YOURS

What things do your family and friends regret spending money on? How do you feel about the ways you spend money?

C 7.02 LISTENING SKILL—Listen for reasons Listen to the panel discussion again. Answer the questions.

1 For what two reasons does Steve regret getting a swimming pool? ______________
2 According to Monica, what are the problems with vacation homes? ______________
____
3 Why does Omar regret buying a desktop computer? ______________
4 Why does Sarah say she wishes she hadn't spent money on dolls? ______________

D IN GROUPS THINKING SKILL—Analyze After listening to the panel discussion, what can you infer about people's reasons for buying things that they later regret? Why do so many people waste money on those things?

PRONUNCIATION /s/ and /z/

A 7.03 Do the letters in bold make an /s/ sound or a /z/ sound? Listen and check. Then practice saying the words.

lose waste tools use exercise house desktop objects

GRAMMAR past perfect for wishes about the past

A Choose the correct options.

1 "We really wish we had never bought that vacation home!" means ...
   a "We bought a vacation home."
   b "We didn't buy a vacation home."

2 "I really wish I had saved that money instead" means ...
   a "I saved money."
   b "I didn't save money."

3 The correct form of the verb for a wish about the past is *had* (*not/never*) + ...
   a past participle.
   b base form.

For more practice, go to page 152.

B Write what the person probably wishes in each situation. You may want to write more than one sentence.

1 Justin bought a motorcycle two years ago. Since then, he has had three accidents and a lot of hospital bills.
   a He wishes he hadn't *bought the motorcycle.*
   b He wishes he had *been more careful.*

2 Karen sold her house and moved to another town. It's expensive there, and she is paying more for rent than she was paying for her mortgage loan.
   a Karen wishes she had ______________________.
   b Karen wishes she hadn't ______________________.

3 Paul got a good job offer, so he quit college and took the job. Now he is worried that he won't be able to move forward in his career.
   a Paul wishes he had ______________________.
   b Paul wishes he hadn't ______________________.

4 Leo is 45, and he is losing his hair. He saw an ad on TV for a machine that makes hair grow. It was expensive, but he ordered it immediately because he didn't want to waste any time. He didn't read any reviews of the product. He has been using the machine for several months, but the machine doesn't work.
   a Leo wishes he had ______________________.
   b Leo wishes he hadn't ______________________.

C IN PAIRS Read your sentences from B. Did you have similar ideas? Discuss.

SPEAKING

A Think of two or three things you wish you hadn't bought. Use the cues to make notes about each thing.

Object or service bought: ______________________
Reason(s) you bought it: ______________________
Reason(s) why you regret buying it: ______________________

B IN GROUPS Tell your group about the things you regret buying. Use the Confident Communicator box to help you.

CONFIDENT COMMUNICATOR
KEEP TALKING

To give reasons for opinions and decisions, use the following phrases:
One reason why I wish ... is that ...
I should/shouldn't have ... because ...
The problem is/was that ...
I wish I had ... before I ...

LESSON 3 Life's Regrets

LISTENING

A **THINKING SKILL—Apply** **As a class, predict five things you think people often regret when they get older.**

1 ______________________________
2 ______________________________
3 ______________________________
4 ______________________________
5 ______________________________

B **7.04** **Listen to a talk about regrets. Which of your ideas in A does the speaker mention? Did any of the regrets surprise you?**

C **7.05 LISTENING SKILL—Listen for main ideas** **Listen again to three segments of the talk about types of regrets. Then choose the main idea of each segment.**

1 Professional Lives
   a People wish they had earned more money.
   b People wish they had not worked so much.

2 Friendships
   a People wish they hadn't lost touch with old friends.
   b People wish they hadn't made old friends angry.

3 Children
   a People wish they had taught their children to do more things.
   b People wish they had had more children.

VOCABULARY collocations

A **Match the parts of the verb phrases.**

1 turn down ____
2 miss ____
3 get in / stay in / lose ____
4 spend / waste ____
5 break up with ____

a a job / an invitation / an opportunity / a chance
b a boyfriend / girlfriend
c an opportunity / a chance
d touch (with someone)
e time or money

B **Complete the paragraph with the correct forms of verb phrases from A.**

I'm 84 years old, and I've had a wonderful life, but I have a few regrets. I've **1** _____missed_____ some _____chances_____ to do exciting things and make my life even better. I also have a professional regret. I **2** ____________ an ____________ to go to an excellent art school because I didn't want to move to New York, and I really regret that. I stayed in my small town and lived with my parents. I **3** ____________ some ____________ (about three years) doing small jobs before I finally went to college. I wish I had gone to college and started my studies earlier. Finally, one of my biggest regrets is that I didn't **4** ____________ with my best friend from college, but I'm trying to **5** ____________ with her now. I hope I can find her.

MAKE IT REAL

There are many ways to describe the end of a relationship. People can *split up with* or *part ways with* their partners.

WRITING

A **IN PAIRS** **Read the blog entry. Why does the writer have mixed feelings about the messages?**

NO REGRETS? Really?

There are many messages on posters and on the internet that tell us that we should never regret things we think we should or shouldn't have done. **They say that** we should follow our hearts, take chances, and do the things we really want to do. That way, when we are older, we will not think "I wish I had done X," or "I wish I hadn't done Y." **Another argument is that** we should only regret the things we *wanted* to do but didn't do.

I have mixed feelings about these messages. **I think** people sometimes have to take chances in order to reach their goals. **I believe that** people often waste time regretting decisions they made and thinking about what they should have done differently. However, it is unrealistic to think that people can live their whole lives with no regrets. We all have regrets about something.

B **Write the phrases in bold in A in the correct columns in the table.**

Stating Your Opinion	Stating Other People's Opinions
In my opinion, …	Some people say that …
In my experience, …	Other people believe that …
I feel that …	Others feel that …
______________	______________
______________	______________
______________	

C **Think about the posters and blog in A. Make notes in your notebook.**

1 What is your opinion of the first poster? Why?
2 What is your opinion of the second poster? Why?
3 What is your opinion of the blog? Do you agree or disagree with the blogger's ideas? Why?

D **Write a blog about your opinion on regrets. Include phrases from B.**

E **IN GROUPS** **Read your blog to your group. What are your group members' opinions about your ideas?**

SPEAKING

A **Make notes to tell an anecdote about a small thing that you regret. Try to think of something funny if possible. You do not have to talk about any regrets that you feel uncomfortable about.**

- What did you do or say?
- What was the result?
- What do you wish you had done differently?
- What did you learn from the experience?

B **IN GROUPS** **Tell your anecdotes. Give your classmates further advice about what they should or shouldn't have done. Use the Confident Communicator box to help you.**

Last week, I was at a restaurant with some friends. We ordered so much food! For dessert, I asked for a "chocolate bomb." It was a huge slice of chocolate cake with a massive serving of chocolate ice cream. I ate all of it, but felt so sick later. I definitely wish I hadn't eaten that dessert! I should have ordered some fruit.

CONFIDENT COMMUNICATOR
START TALKING

To start a story, set the scene.
Place: *I was at / in / on my way to …*
People: *I was alone / with …*
What was happening: *I was / We were … –ing …*

Language and Life

Interpersonal Communication – A Presentation

A 7.06 **Read the case study. Then choose the correct options on the next page.**

Case Study:

The Edsel

INTRODUCTION

In 1957, the Ford Motor Company introduced the Edsel, a car that they were promoting as "the car of the future." However, the Edsel turned out to be one of the greatest mistakes in business history.

BASIC IDEA AND RESEARCH

- In the early 1950s, the US economy was extremely strong, and Ford wanted a new car in the medium-price range. Unfortunately, they did not pay attention to research that showed the US would soon experience a recession.
- Ford did not do enough research to find out what customers really wanted in a car. Instead, they based most of their decisions on the opinions of Ford executives, the people who managed the company.
- The executives spent a lot of money on research to help them decide on the name of the car, but they decided to use the name of Henry Ford's son, Edsel. It turned out that people hated the name.

DESIGN

- Ford wanted to design a car that looked very different from existing cars, but the company did not do research to find out if people liked the design. They didn't show the design to sales people or the public before the car was produced.
- The company wanted to produce a car that many different types of people would buy, so they made 18 different models of the Edsel.
- The Edsel had many new features that hadn't been used in cars before, but those new things did not always work well.

DESIGN

- Ford started promoting the Edsel as "the car of the future" in advertisements a year before the car was produced. There was a lot of excitement about it, and people even waited in line to see it. Unfortunately, many people did not like the new design when they saw it. They decided that it was an ugly, expensive car with a terrible name.

1957 Edsel

1964 Mustang

LESSONS LEARNED

Ford learned from its mistakes with the Edsel. They did excellent research for the Ford Mustang, which they produced in the 1960s. The Ford Mustang became one of the greatest successes in business history. It was exactly the right car for the right customers at the right time, and the Mustang is still a very popular car today.

1 The basic idea for the Edsel was based on …
   a existing cars. b Ford executives' opinions. c a lot of research.
2 Ford wanted to sell the Edsel to …
   a young people. b wealthy people. c many types of people.
3 To sell the Edsel, Ford used the idea that it was …
   a modern and different. b inexpensive. c attractive.
4 People thought the Edsel was _____ it had appeared in the advertisements.
   a better than b not as good as c the same as
5 Ford used _____ process for designing the Mustang.
   a exactly the same b a similar c a completely different

B IN PAIRS Discuss the questions.

1 What should Ford have done differently when it designed, promoted, and produced the Edsel?
2 Why was the Mustang a great success?

C IN GROUPS You are going to work together to plan a presentation about a product that was a failure. Follow the steps. Think about each person's skills and what each person can do to prepare and deliver the presentation. Look at the different points below and decide who in your group should be responsible for each part.

Step 1

Research the product—who likes investigating new facts?

- name and type of product
- company that made it
- target customers
- where it was advertised
- what the advertising promised
- design or quality
- how it was promoted
- the product
- how it was advertised
- what the company and others can learn from this experience

Step 2

Structure the presentation—who likes organizing information in an interesting and logical way?

- Decide the basic structure of the presentation.
- Plan what information there should be in each part.
- Agree on the key point you want to communicate.

Step 3

Give the presentation—who likes talking to groups and communicating their ideas?

- Decide who will say what.
- Discuss how you can engage your audience.
- Give the presentation!

D Discuss the questions.

1 How did you communicate your reasons for choosing each person's responsibility?
2 Did everyone agree with the reasons? Why or why not?
3 In what other situations might you have to communicate with a group of people?

MAKE IT DIGITAL

Before you buy a product, go online and read customer reviews. This can help you decide whether or not to spend money on the product.

VOCABULARY review

SCORE: / 10

A Complete the text with the correct forms of the verbs from the box.

find out	look into	lose touch	spend	turn out
go up	lose	miss	stay in touch	waste

My dad's business wasn't growing, so he **1** ______________ why that was happening, and he **2** ______________ that the main problem was customer service. When the company started, my dad personally **3** ______________ with all of the customers, but as the company grew, he had many other things to do. He said he couldn't **4** ______________ time visiting or talking on the phone to customers. It **5** ______________ that if you don't take care of your customers, you **6** ______________ their business! So he hired some people to help with other parts of the business, and he spoke directly with customers. Now he doesn't **7** ______________ an opportunity to talk to a customer. He **8** ______________ a lot of time each day making phone calls, and he often visits customers. He never **9** ______________ with them! Now my dad's business is growing again! Profits have **10** ______________ and he is happy.

GRAMMAR review

SCORE: / 10

A For each situation, write two sentences: one using *should / shouldn't have* and another using *wish*. Use your notebook.

1 My dad's new cell phone isn't very good. He didn't read any reviews before he bought it.
2 I didn't go to Sam's party last Friday. I heard it was great!
3 Monica didn't help her brother study for his math exam, and he failed it.
4 I moved to another town and lost touch with my old friends.
5 Carol and Steve bought 20 lottery tickets, but they didn't win. They wasted a lot of money!

16–20 correct: You can talk about past mistakes and regrets. You can use *should/shouldn't have* and the past perfect for wishes about the past.
0–15 correct: Look again at the Vocabulary and Grammar sections in the unit.

TOTAL SCORE: / 20

WHAT DO YOU KNOW NOW? Look back at page 67 and add the words you know now to the box.

STUDY SKILLS STRUCTURING YOUR WRITING

Take the quiz about structuring your writing. Go to **Study Skills** on page 133 to find the answers. Then learn more about structuring your writing.

1 When we use the word *argument* to talk about essay writing, what do we mean?
a a disagreement between the writer and the reader
b the point the writer makes (which also gives the essay its structure)

2 Put the essay outline in order.
_____ main argument
_____ introduction
_____ conclusion
_____ objections to main argument
_____ title

3 Which of the following are linking words?
a although **b** in spite of **c** consequently **d** outline

UNIT 8 A New Home?

WHAT DO YOU ALREADY KNOW?

1 Think of words you know about space. Write the words.

2 IN PAIRS Share and compare your ideas. Add more words to your lists.

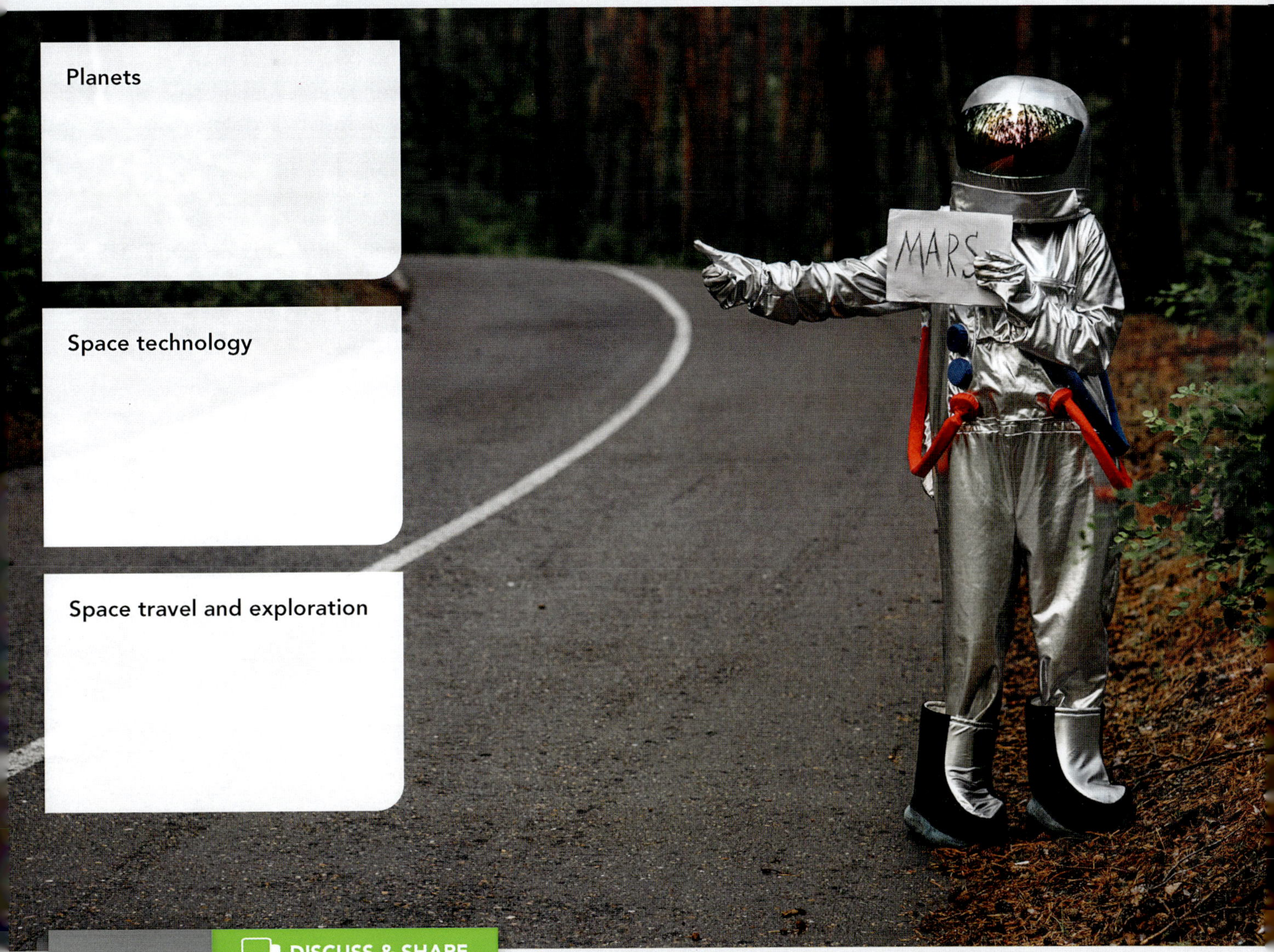

Planets

Space technology

Space travel and exploration

VIDEO

DISCUSS & SHARE

3 IN GROUPS Watch the video and answer the question.

SYM Should we focus on problems on Earth before we explore other planets?

In this unit, you will ...

- talk about hypothetical events in history, role play an interview with an astronaut, and discuss your opinions of space exploration.
- use thinking skills: analyze, question, and recall.
- read about the extinction of the dinosaurs.
- use strategies and language to express possibility or probability, use indirect questions to sound more polite, and clarify reasons for opinions.
- use reasoning skills to make decisions about a space team.
- follow an astrobiologist to learn about this job and the skills needed for this industry.

VOCABULARY

A Match the words to the definitions.

asteroid debris crater tidal wave extinction soot herbivore carnivore

1 ______________: a very large wave
2 ______________: a dirty black substance from a fire
3 ______________: an animal that eats only plants
4 ______________: a mass of rock that moves in space
5 ______________: when a species disappears
6 ______________: a large round hole in the ground
7 ______________: an animal that eats other animals
8 ______________: small pieces left when something is destroyed

READING

A IN PAIRS READING SKILL – Predict Number the events leading up to the extinction of the dinosaurs in the order you think they happened.

☐ Plants died, and the herbivores didn't have food.

☐ Burning debris caused forest fires.

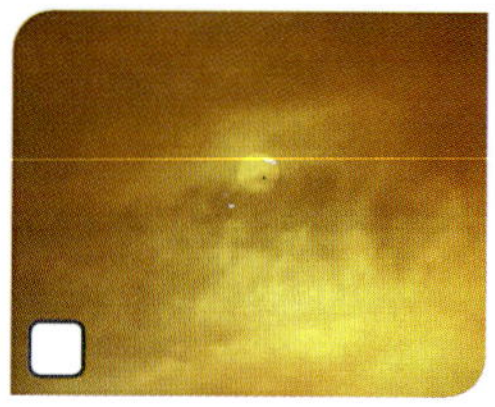
☐ Soot blocked the sunlight.

1 An asteroid hit the Earth and made a crater.

☐ The carnivores didn't have food, so they died.

☐ The impact caused tidal waves.

B 8.01 Read the article and check your predictions.

WHAT ON EARTH HAPPENED?

Sixty-six million years ago, during the time of the dinosaurs, something happened that changed our planet forever. A meteorite hit the Earth near the Yucatan Peninsula of Mexico and created a crater that was 185 km wide. The impact caused an explosion equal to about 10 million Hiroshima bombs. This caused a chain of events that resulted in mass extinctions of life on Earth.

Scientists almost all agree that the meteorite was the main cause of these mass extinctions. They now think they understand what happened after the meteorite hit. First, if you had been within 1,000 km. of the impact site, you would have been killed by a massive ball of fire. Almost immediately after the impact, there were earthquakes and 300-meter-high tidal waves all over the planet. About eight minutes after the impact, debris from the explosion would have started to fall out of the sky. A lot of the debris was on fire, and this caused massive forest fires. A few minutes later, there would have been 965-km-per-hour winds caused by the quickly heating air. These winds would have destroyed everything they came into contact with.

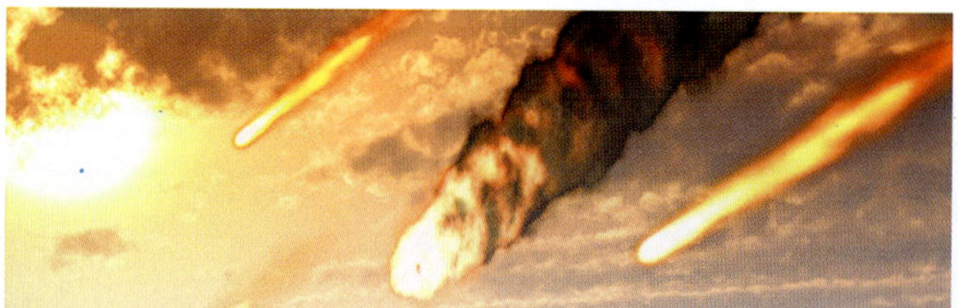

Common theories suggest that if you had been far enough away, you would have survived the explosion. However, in a few days, you would have seen the sky get very dark because of the carbon soot that filled the atmosphere. The soot blocked the sunlight for months and perhaps for years. Without sunlight, plants began to die. When the plants died, there was no food for the herbivores, so they died, too. When the herbivores died, the carnivores didn't have food, so they also died.

It is interesting to try to imagine what would have happened if the meteorite had *not* crashed into Earth. Some scientists think dinosaurs might have survived. They believe they could have adapted to slow changes in climate over many years. Just imagine ...

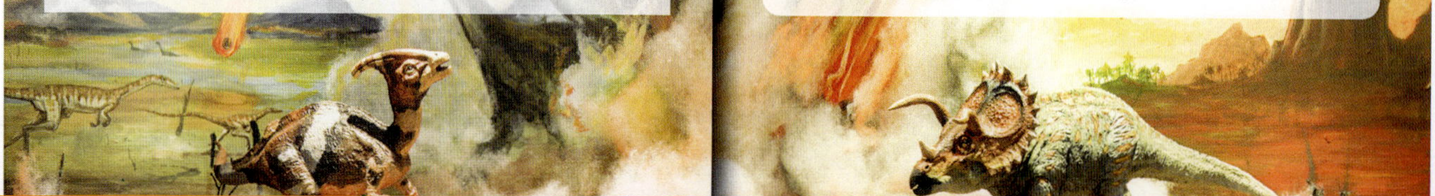

C IN GROUPS THINKING SKILL—Analyze Infer the answers to these questions. Explain the reasons for your answers.

1 Did all life on Earth disappear after the asteroid crashed?
2 Do all scientists agree on what caused the dinosaurs to become extinct?

GRAMMAR third conditional

A Choose the sentences with the same meanings. Then choose the correct options in the rule.

1 First, if you had been within 1,000 km of the impact site, …
  a You were not within 1,000 km of the impact site.
  b You were within 1,000 km of the impact site.
2 If you had been far enough away, you would have survived the explosion.
  a Your survival in the past was certain.
  b Your survival in the past was not certain.
3 …. others think dinosaurs might have survived.
  a The dinosaurs' survival in the past was certain.
  b The dinosaurs' survival in the past was not certain.
4 … they could have adapted to slow changes in climate over many years.
  a Their adaptation was certain.
  b Their adaptation was not certain.

To make the third conditional, use *if* + present / past perfect and *would/might/could have* + present / past participle.

For more practice, go to page 152.

B Write third conditional sentences for the situations.

1 A meteorite hit the Earth. The dinosaurs didn't survive.
If a meteorite hadn't hit the Earth, the dinosaurs might have survived.
2 There were no humans on the Earth at that time. They didn't die from the meteorite crash.
______
3 The soot in the air blocked the sun. Temperatures became much cooler.
______
4 Dinosaurs didn't have food after the meteorite crashed. They disappeared in a few years.
______

C IN PAIRS Take turns reading your sentences. Did you have similar ideas?

SPEAKING

A IN PAIRS How would history have been different if certain events had or had not happened? Write down three examples in your notebook.

If the 1969 moon landing hadn't been successful, people might not have gone to the moon again.

B IN GROUPS Share your ideas. Discuss whether you agree with your classmates' speculations. Use the Confident Communicator box to help you.

CONFIDENT COMMUNICATOR
KEEP TALKING

To express possibility or probability, use *maybe* or *probably*:
Maybe humans wouldn't have gone to the moon again if the moon landing hadn't been successful. (possibility)
Humans probably wouldn't have gone to the moon again if the moon landing hadn't been successful. (probability)

Life in Space

VOCABULARY space

A Complete the sentences with the words from the box.

outer space | International Space Station | space capsule | spacecraft | space shuttle | zero gravity

1 People have been traveling into space on ______________ for over fifty years.
2 The first person who traveled to ______________, the area outside Earth's atmosphere, was Yuri Gagarin, in 1961.
3 In the 1970s, the first ______________ was developed, a vehicle that could go to space and return several times.
4 A ______________ is a compartment or cabin where the astronauts live during a space flight.
5 In the 1990s, the US, Russia, Japan, and Europe built the ______________ (ISS) to discover more about human life in space.
6 One of the effects of living in ______________ is that people get taller!

LISTENING

A IN PAIRS **What do you think the challenges of living in a space capsule would be? Discuss.**

B 8.02 **Listen to an interview about life in space. Were your ideas correct?**

C 8.02 LISTENING SKILL—Listen for specific information **Listen again and complete the notes.**

1. *Number of times Karen has flown into space:*
2. *Number of times she has been to the International Space Station (ISS):*
3. *How you sit down in space:*
4. *Why Karen has short hair:*
5. *Where spacecraft may go in the future:*
6. *What the Earth looks like from outer space:*

D IN GROUPS THINKING SKILL—Question **Decide what the astronaut meant when she made this statement about observing Earth from outer space.**

"You can see the oceans and the continents, but no countries, of course, and that can make you think differently about our world."

MAKE IT REAL

The International Space Station is often referred to as the *ISS*. It is common in English to refer to companies and institutions by their initials. Can you think of any more examples?

PRONUNCIATION consonant clusters with /s/

A 8.03 **Underline the consonant cluster with /s/ in each word. Listen and practice.**

1 ho<u>st</u> 2 guest 3 space 4 sleep 5 just 6 school 7 student 8 desk

GRAMMAR indirect questions

A Read the examples of direct and indirect questions and complete the rules with the correct options.

Direct questions	Indirect questions
What is life like at zero gravity?	Can you tell us what life is like at zero gravity?
How do you drink water?	Could you explain how you drink water?
Will the US have space shuttles again in the future?	Do you know if/whether the US will have space shuttles again in the future?

1 Direct questions have the verb *be* or the auxiliary (*will*, *did*, etc.) **before** / **after** the subject.
2 Indirect questions have the main verb **before** / **after** the subject.
3 Indirect questions in the simple present or simple past **have** / **don't have** the auxiliary *do*/*did*.

For more practice, go to page 153.

B Rewrite the direct questions as indirect questions.

1 How big is the International Space Station?
Could you tell me ______________________________?
2 What do astronauts in the ISS do?
Can you explain ______________________________?
3 Will the ISS ever return to Earth?
Do you think ______________________________?

C IN GROUPS Take turns asking and answering the questions from B.

SPEAKING

A IN PAIRS Read the facts and look at your notes from LISTENING C. Use the information in the web page and your own ideas to think of questions to ask an astronaut. Include indirect questions.

ZERO GRAVITY FACTS

- You lose muscle mass, so you have to exercise a lot to build muscles.
- You breathe in things that are floating in the air, so you have to be careful about things like crumbs from food, drops of water, or hair from shaving.
- It's hard to sleep. You have to sleep in a special sleeping bag with arm bags so that your arms don't float.

B IN PAIRS Role-play your interview for another pair. Use the Confident Communicator box to help you.

A: Can you tell me what you like and don't like about life in space?
B: Well, I really like … I don't like … or … very much because … .
A: That's interesting. And do you know if you will go to space again?

CONFIDENT COMMUNICATOR
KEEP TALKING

To make a question sound more polite, especially in a formal situation like an interview, use at least some indirect questions: *Can you tell me why you didn't like the experience?* Instead of *Why didn't you like the experience?*

LESSON 3 Do We Need Space Exploration?

LISTENING

A IN GROUPS Discuss the reasons for space exploration. How many different things do space programs do?

B 8.04 LISTENING SKILL—Listen for main ideas Listen to a panel discussion about space exploration. Then answer the questions.

1 Are the people on the panel in favor of or against space exploration?

____

2 What does Seth, the astronaut, say space exploration is mainly about?

____

3 What does the second guest, Lauren, say that satellites do?

____

4 What does the third speaker, Cristina, focus on in her comments?

____

5 What does the last speaker, Mike, say the space program is like?

____

C 8.04 THINKING SKILL—Recall Choose the speaker who discussed each point. Compare with a partner. Then listen and check.

1 The space program encourages young people to study. Seth / Lauren / Cristina / Mike
2 The space program gave us cell phone cameras. Seth / Lauren / Cristina / Mike
3 The space program makes us safer. Seth / Lauren / Cristina / Mike
4 The space program is not only about astronauts. Seth / Lauren / Cristina / Mike

VOCABULARY space program inventions

A Label the pictures with words from the box.

cordless vacuum	foil blanket	home insulation
memory foam	water filter	wireless headset

1 
____

2 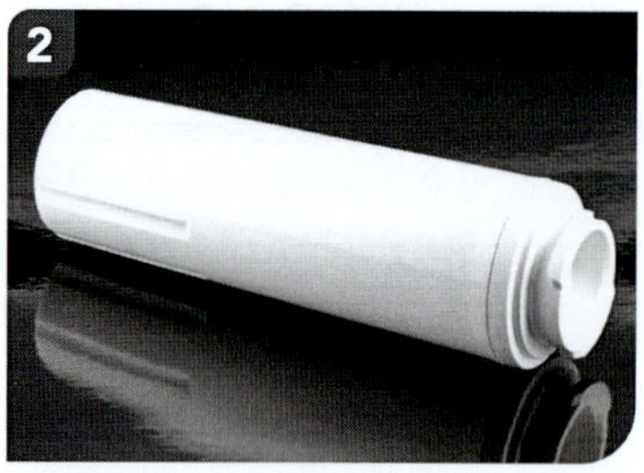
____

3 
____

4 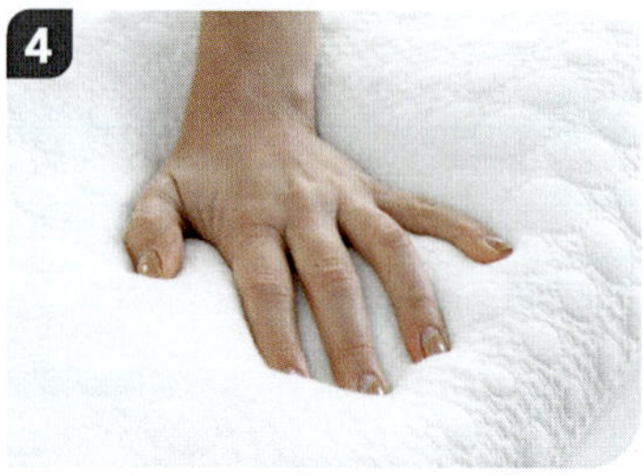
____

5 
____

6 
____

B IN GROUPS Discuss which of the contributions from space exploration you have used.

WRITING

A Read the opinion posted on a blog site. Then choose the statements that best reflect the writer's opinion.

Stop Exploring Space!

It's time to stop exploring space. It is true that space exploration has developed technology that is used in many ways on Earth. However, I feel certain that if the technology hadn't been invented for the space program, it would have been invented anyway. The main problem with space exploration is the cost. If we hadn't spent billions of dollars on space exploration, we could have already stopped world hunger. In addition, space travel is dangerous. Astronauts become ill from a number of health problems from being in zero gravity for long periods of time. Furthermore, we don't know what dangerous viruses might be in space—it could be dangerous for Planet Earth. Also, some kinds of rockets use enormous amounts of fossil fuel.

Many people argue that we need to learn about our universe. Nevertheless, I am convinced that we should spend our energy and our money on ways to make our lives better here on Earth.

1 a He thinks that we wouldn't have had some technologies if we hadn't had a space program.
b He thinks we would have developed our technologies even without a space program.
2 a He thinks we should spend money to stop world hunger instead of on space exploration.
b He thinks we have almost stopped world hunger.
3 a He thinks being in space is very dangerous.
b He thinks people will live in space in the near future.
4 a He thinks we should look for new sources of fossil fuel on other planets.
b He thinks space exploration uses too much fossil fuel.

B Look back at the blog. Find words and phrases that connect ideas.

To add ideas: *and*, ____________, ____________, ____________
To contrast ideas: *but*, ____________, ____________

C You are going to respond to the blog with the opposite point of view. Write notes to plan your response.

Opening statement: ____________
Arguments from the blog you disagree with: ____________
Other reasons to support space exploration: ____________
Closing statement: ____________

D Write your blog post. Use connecting words and phrases from B to structure your response.

E IN PAIRS Read each other's blog posts. Did you use similar arguments?

SPEAKING

A Decide whether you are for or against space exploration in the future. Make a list of your arguments. Use ideas from this lesson or your own ideas.

B IN GROUPS Discuss your opinions from A. Ask questions to clarify your classmates' reasons for their opinions. Use the Confident Communicator box to help you.

A: I think space exploration is a waste of time.
B: Can you tell me why you think that?

CONFIDENT COMMUNICATOR
KEEP TALKING

To ask someone to clarify the reasons for their opinions, use these phrases:
Can you tell me why you think …?
Why do you think …?
What makes you believe …?

Language and Life

Reason Effectively – Space Team

A IN PAIRS What challenges/problems/difficulties would people living on Mars face? Discuss.

B 8.05 Read the description of what life would be like on Mars. Does it include any of your ideas from A? What other challenges does it include?

Life on Mars

Artist's rendition of an ecosystem on Mars.

Traveling to Mars is hard. Living on Mars is even harder. First, there are serious environmental issues. One problem is radiation. Astronauts on the International Space Station get 10 times more radiation than on Earth, and the radiation in deep space could be even stronger. One possible solution is ice-covered domes because ice partly blocks radiation. The second problem is the effects of low gravity on the human body. People's bones and muscles become weaker if they are in low gravity for a long time. It is necessary to use weights and do heavy exercise to prevent this. A third problem is that people will have to live in a closed ecosystem. They have to stay inside a dome or a spacesuit at all times. There is no fresh air, so there is a danger of pollution or contamination by bacteria or viruses.

Life on Mars will also have psychological difficulties. First, there will be very few people on Mars, at least at the beginning, so there will not be many choices of friends. There will be no restaurants, cafés, or parks, so there will be few options for social activities, and life could be very boring. Second, the living spaces will be very small. People will be living very close to each other. Life will not be very comfortable. Water will be very limited, so people will have to take 30-second showers and almost never wash their clothes. Plants cannot grow on Mars, so all food will be dried or in cans. Also, most food tastes the same at low gravity. Finally, communication with Earth will be very hard. Cell phones and other voice communications will be impossible, so the only communication will be through email. It will take 20 minutes for an email to reach Earth, and another 20 minutes to get a reply, and most of us are used to very fast communication with our friends and families.

C IN GROUPS You are going to choose the first three people who will live on Mars for two years. What characteristics and experience are important? Make a list.

Characteristics	Experience
calm	*background in science*

D IN GROUPS Read the descriptions of the candidates for the Mars mission. Analyze and evaluate each description. Discuss the characteristics and experience you listed in C and relate them to each candidate. Consider the candidates' pros and cons and choose the best candidate.

MARTIN
MALE, 28
USA
COMEDIAN
NOT MARRIED

Competes in sports competitions and marathons. Now doing a TV show where he uses humor to teach people about nutrition. Very friendly, but friends say he talks too much!

Specializes in rare tropical diseases. Has lived in the jungles of northern Colombia and central Africa. Lived by herself for a year on a remote Pacific island. No time to do sports or socialize with people because her work is so important.

SUSANA
FEMALE, 45
COLOMBIA
MEDICAL RESEARCHER
NOT MARRIED

ARI
MALE, 35
RUSSIA
DOCTOR
MARRIED

Works at a family medicine clinic in Moscow. Practices general medicine, but specializes in respiratory diseases in children. Grows vegetables and rides his bicycle in his free time. Work and city living make him feel stressed; he relaxes by walking and bicycling in the countryside on weekends. Wife and two children support his decision to go to Mars for two years.

Designs large urban office buildings and specializes in green buildings with solar energy, rainwater collection systems, and air pollution cleaning systems. Loves decorating; skilled at house repairs. Loves living in Nairobi because it's an exciting city with many things to do. Has many friends and a very active social life. Married for two years; hopes to have children in the future.

ASHA
FEMALE, 32
KENYA
ARCHITECT
MARRIED

CLAUDIA
FEMALE, 50
BRAZIL
PSYCHIATRIST
MARRIED

Specializes in stress disorders. Uses herbs, meditation, and exercise therapy to help her patients. Works well with patients because she has had a lot of stress in the past. Grows her own herbs. Learned about herbal medicine when she lived in a small village in the Amazon where there was no electricity, running water, or communication with the outside world.

E IN GROUPS As a class, discuss which candidates you chose and which factors—experience, skills, other factors—most influenced your group's decision about the candidates.

A: Can you explain why you think Susana is better than Ari?

B: Susana has more experience with unusual diseases. If Ari had done more research on those types of diseases, he would have been a better candidate than Susana, but I think her experience is important.

F Which factors most influenced your group's decision about the candidates—experience or skills? Did any other factors, such as gender, age, or nationality influence your decision? If so, which ones?

G Discuss the questions.

1. What process did your group use to evaluate and select the three candidates? Were you happy with the process?
2. What steps are necessary in order to reason effectively?
3. How do reasoning skills help you at college or at work?

MAKE IT DIGITAL

Do research to find out about someone who went on a space mission. What skills did they have?

VOCABULARY review

SCORE: / 10

A Complete the sentences with words from the box.

asteroid	cordless vacuums	debris	extinction	ISS
outer space	soot	spacecraft	tidal waves	zero gravity

Millions of years ago, a/an **1** ______ hit the Earth and caused the **2** ______ of many species of animals and plants. The impact caused giant **3** ______ from the ocean and fires that filled the air with black, smoky **4** ______.

People started traveling into **5** ______ in the 1960s, and now people from different countries live on the **6** ______ for months at a time. Astronauts travel there in a Russian **7** ______. It is hard to live at **8** ______ because everything floats. If there is any **9** ______ in the air, it can get into the air filters and damage them. Space programs have given us many everyday inventions, like memory foam, home insulation, and **10** ______.

GRAMMAR review

SCORE: / 10

A Write the correct verb forms to make third conditional sentences. More than one answer may be possible.

1. If a meteorite ______ (not hit) Earth, maybe the dinosaurs ______ (live) for longer.
2. If the meteorite ______ (hit) the Earth more recently, people ______ (die).
3. My uncle ______ (be) an astronaut if he ______ (grow up) in the US.
4. If I ______ (know) about last night's TV show on space programs, I ______ (watch) it.

B Rewrite the direct questions as indirect questions in your notebook.

1. Are there any good documentaries about space exploration?
2. How big is the International Space Station?
3. Where did the meteorite hit?
4. Why did mammals survive after the meteorite?
5. Have other meteorites hit the Earth?
6. Will we live on other planets in the future?

16–20 correct: You can talk about events in the past and their impact on today. You can ask questions and discuss space exploration. You can use the third conditional and make indirect questions.
0–15 correct: Look again at the Vocabulary and Grammar sections in the unit.

TOTAL SCORE: / 20

WHAT DO YOU KNOW NOW? Look back at page 77 and add the words you know now to the boxes.

FOLLOW A PRO SPACE

Take the quiz about space. Go to Follow A Pro on page 134 to find the answers. Then learn about astrobiology.

1 The hottest planet in our solar system is …
a Mercury. **b** Venus. **c** Mars.

2 Scientists think there may be a planet made of …
a diamonds. **b** gold. **c** silver.

3 One day on Venus is longer than one … on Earth.
a week **b** month **c** year

4 A NASA space suit costs about … dollars.
a five hundred thousand **b** one million **c** twelve million

UNIT 9

The World of News

WHAT DO YOU ALREADY KNOW?

1 Think of words you know about media and the news. Write the words.

2 **IN PAIRS** Share and compare your ideas. Add more words to your lists.

Media/News

VIDEO

DISCUSS & SHARE

3 **IN GROUPS** Watch the video and answer the question.

SYM The news—how much is too much?

In this unit, you will ...

- give your opinions on fake news, journalists and citizen journalists, compare real and fake news stories, and role-play a job interview for a news career.
- use thinking skills: analyze, apply, and deduce.
- read about developments in news.
- use strategies and language to ask for an opinion, interrupt politely, and introduce new information about your skills and experience.
- use problem-solving skills to discuss the pros and cons of solutions to a problem.
- learn tips to make notes.

LESSON 1 News in the 21st Century

READING

A How interested are you in the news? Share your view with the class.

1 Very interested. I like to know what's happening in the world.
2 Pretty interested. Some things interest me more than others.
3 Not interested at all. Events in the news aren't really part of my life.

B 9.01 READING SKILL—Identify text types Read the texts. Write the correct text type from the box next to each text. There is one text type you do not need.

blog post | email | online article | review | tweet

Changing Times

It's no surprise that newspaper sales have fallen in recent years and TV news audiences are smaller because of the **effect** of 24/7 online news sites. It's too early to say how this will affect the way we present the news, but it's such an important **industry** that it's likely to survive technological change. There will always be journalism and a need for good journalists.

1 ______________________

I never buy newspapers these days. What's the point? News is reported so quickly because it changes all the time. I'm not that interested in current affairs, but I read news stories online, and sometimes I watch the news on TV if something "big" is happening somewhere in the world. I see some news items on social media, but the majority are **human-interest stories**, and that kind of story is not interesting enough for me to repost. I'd like to know if anyone here does repost those stories in their newsfeed.
posted by jamiek 12:23

follow

2 ______________________

Citizen Journalists: The Word on the Street
by Amos Hadfield

A must-read for all journalism students is *Citizen Journalists: The Word on the Street* by Amos Hadfield. Citizen journalism is where ordinary people collect, report, share, and comment on news stories via their social media newsfeeds or tweets. It's an interesting **trend** because it's so hard to control. A positive point is that ordinary people can get involved. However, there are some problems. "It isn't easy to limit the spread of fake news" he writes. "**Governments** want more power, but that is also dangerous."

3 ______________________

Amber Spratt @ The Ark

Breaking news! People are here in the thousands—there's such an amazing atmosphere right now. No word from the president yet, but we expect more information soon. #excitingtimes

4 ______________________

GLOSSARY

journalism (n): the activity of reporting the news
fake (adj): not real or true
current affairs (phrase): events that are happening now and that are discussed in news reports

C Read the texts in B again. Complete the sentences with the correct text types.

1 The writer of the ______________ is not interested in the news.
2 The writer of the ______________ is reporting events as they happen.
3 The writer of the ______________ believes that journalism is an important profession.
4 The writer of the ______________ mentions a new way of reporting news.

D THINKING SKILL—Analyze Read text 3 in B again. Compare the arguments in favor of citizen journalism and the arguments against it.

VOCABULARY

A Match the definitions to a word or phrase in bold in READING B.

1 news reports about a person's life or experiences ______
2 a change that is the result of another action ______
3 a specific trade or service ______
4 the groups of people who control a country ______
5 something popular at a specific time ______

MAKE IT YOURS

Go online and look at a website where you can read the news in English. What news sections does the website have? Look up any words for the sections that you don't know.

GRAMMAR *so, such, too, enough*

A Complete the sentences from the texts in READING B. Then match with the correct forms.

1 It's an interesting trend because ______ to control.
2 … there's ______ right now.
3 … that kind of story is ______.
4 It's ______ how this will affect …

a *such* + adjective + noun ______
b (*not* +) adjective/adverb + *enough* ______
c *so* + adjective/adverb ______
d *too* + adjective/adverb ______

Can you find any more examples in the texts?

B Match the words (1–4) with their meanings (a–d).

1 *such/so* ______
2 *too* ______
3 *enough* ______
4 *not enough* ______

a more than needed
b less than needed
c the right amount
d very

For more practice, go to page 154.

C Rewrite the sentences correctly in your notebook.

1 Some news reports are such shocking I can't watch them.
2 Jake is enough shy to succeed as a journalist.
3 My journalism teacher said I don't have to rewrite my report. It is enough good.
4 I think being a journalist must be so an interesting job.

D IN PAIRS Discuss sentences 1 and 4 in C. Are they true for you?

SPEAKING

A Make notes about how young people see the news in the 21st century. Think about the questions.

- What types of news stories are young people interested in?
- Are there are too many news sources?
- Are journalists professional enough?

B IN PAIRS Write three opinion questions about these topics. Use *too*, *so*, *such*, or *enough* in your questions.

- Fake news
- Journalists
- Citizen journalists

Do you think there is too much fake news?

C Go around the class. Ask different students your questions. Encourage them to give reasons for their opinions. Use the Confident Communicator box to help you.

CONFIDENT COMMUNICATOR
KEEP TALKING

Use these phrases to ask for someone's opinion:
Hi, can/could I ask you some questions about …?
Do you mind if I ask you about …?
Could you answer some questions about …?

VOCABULARY news stories

A Match the underlined words to the correct definitions (a–f).

1 It can be hard to <u>figure out</u> what is fake news. ____
2 If a news <u>headline</u> makes you laugh, it's probably not true! ____
3 We get news from many different <u>sources</u> – newspapers, TV, news websites and social media, for example. ____
4 To <u>prove</u> that a news story is true, compare it to other reports of the story. ____
5 Fake news is not <u>accurate</u> and can be dangerous. ____
6 You should only <u>trust</u> news websites that have a good record of telling the truth. ____

a show that something is true
b people or places we get information from
c understand; find the answer
d the title of a newspaper story
e believe is honest, fair, and reliable
f true; correct; without mistakes

B Complete the sentences with an underlined word from A.

1 The ____________ is "Dangerous Tigers Escape From Zoo!"
2 Which websites do you ____________ for the world news?
3 Can scientists ____________ that there is life on other planets?
4 We need to include information from three ____________ in our report.
5 How do you know this information about national exam results is ____________?
6 It can be difficult to ____________ how to tell a fake news story from a real one.

LISTENING

A 9.02 Listen to Part 1 of a lecture on fake news. Then answer the question.

Why is fake news a "hot topic"? Give two reasons. ______________________________

____

GLOSSARY
rumor (n): information that may or may not be true

B 9.03 LISTENING SKILL—Listen for information order Listen to Part 2 of the lecture. Put the steps in the correct order (1–5).

a Research the person who wrote the story. ____
b Question everything you read online. ____
c Check links to other news stories. ____
d Research where the story comes from. ____
e Check if the story is on other websites. ____

C THINKING SKILL—Apply Think about a news item you saw on social media. Use the information you heard in B to establish if the news was real or fake.

GRAMMAR modals of deduction

A Read the sentences from LISTENING B. Choose the correct option in the rule.

If they haven't written anything else for a source you trust, the article **could** spread fake news.
Think to yourself, "This story **might** be true, but it **may not be** 100% accurate."
Or, "This story **can't be** true because certain details don't seem right."

When talking about deductions in the present, use a modal (+ *not*) + the **base infinitive** / **infinitive with** ***to*** form of the verb.

B **Complete the sentences with words from the box.**

can't could may might must

You're 99% sure the news is fake.	The news **1** ____________ be fake.
You aren't sure if the news is fake or not.	Do you think that story **2** ____________ / **3** ____________ / **4** ____________ be fake?
You're 95% sure the news is true.	The news **5** ____________ be fake.

For more practice, go to page 154.

C **Complete the sentences with the correct modal of deduction. More than one answer may be possible.**

1 Your friend Lola said she would visit you today. There's a knock at the door.
"That ____________ be Lola."

2 You see someone in a store who looks like your cousin Martha. But Martha works abroad as a journalist.
"That ____________ be Martha."

3 You look out of the window. People are carrying open umbrellas.
"It ____________ be raining."

4 You're sure TV news ends at 11 p.m.
"It's midnight. The news ____________ be on TV."

D IN PAIRS **Look at these pictures. What do you think they show? Use modals of deduction to discuss.**

a

b

c

d

This picture must be a …
This might be a …

MAKE IT REAL

You can use *maybe* and *perhaps* instead of *may be*, *could be*, and *might be*:
Maybe it's a/an … *Perhaps they're …*

SPEAKING

A **Read these two news story summaries. Have you heard about them or seen them in the news?**

Story 1:
Some cities around the world now use "silent fireworks" in displays to make the shows more enjoyable for children and less stressful for pets.

Story 2:
A group of penguins is living on an island of ice and plastic waste in the Pacific Ocean.

B IN PAIRS **Work together to decide which might be fake news and which might be true.**

This one can't be a true news story, because …
That one must be fake news, because …

C IN GROUPS **Talk about how you worked out which news story was fake. Use the Confident Communicator box to help you.**

CONFIDENT COMMUNICATOR
REPAIR IT

To interrupt politely, use the following phrases:
Excuse me, can I just interrupt here and say …
Do you mind if I interrupt?
Sorry, can I just add that …

A News Career

VOCABULARY news careers

A **Look at the pictures. Match the careers from the box with the correct pictures.**

foreign correspondent | investigative journalist | news anchor | newspaper editor | photojournalist | reporter | sports journalist | translator

1

2

3

4

5

6

7

8

B **IN PAIRS Talk about what skills a person needs to do each of the jobs.**

A: I think a news anchor needs to feel confident in front of a camera.

B: True. And an investigative journalist must not be afraid to ask hard questions.

PRONUNCIATION /ə/ versus /r/

A **9.04 There are differences in the pronunciation of certain sounds in British English and American English. Listen and notice the difference between the sounds /ə/ and /r/ at the end of these words.**

1 anch<u>or</u> **2** translat<u>or</u> **3** edit<u>or</u> **4** report<u>er</u>

B **9.05 Listen and choose the sound you hear.**

1 anchor **a** the /ə/ sound **b** the /r/ sound
2 translator **a** the /ə/ sound **b** the /r/ sound
3 editor **a** the /ə/ sound **b** the /r/ sound
4 reporter **a** the /ə/ sound **b** the /r/ sound

LISTENING

A **What do you think the job of foreign correspondent is like? How about a translator in a different country?**

B **9.06 Listen to the interview and choose the correct answers.**

1 What is Dana McDonald's job?
a foreign correspondent **b** translator **c** professor
2 Where does Dana McDonald live?
a England **b** the US **c** India
3 What did Peter Marsden study at college?
a Arabic **b** English and French **c** journalism
4 Where is Peter from?
a the US **b** Algeria **c** India

C 9.06 LISTENING SKILL—Listen for opinions **Listen again and decide who expresses the following opinions. Write *D* for Dana, *P* for Peter, or *B* for both.**

Who …

1 worked in a different career in the beginning? ____
2 finds their job quite hard? ____
3 doesn't really speak the language of the country they live in? ____
4 is away from home for long periods of time? ____
5 works for themselves? ____

MAKE IT REAL

To talk about a job that would/ wouldn't suit you, use:
I'd make a good/terrible … because I …
e.g., *I'd make a terrible photojournalist because I can't take good pictures!*

D THINKING SKILL—Deduce **Decide what you would find challenging about being a foreign correspondent or a translator in a different country.**

WRITING

A Read this fact file about a person who works as an undercover investigative journalist. Would you like to do a job like this?

FACT FILE: Undercover investigative journalist
NAME: Faye Garcia [not her real name]
AGE: 32

I work as an undercover journalist. I hide my real identity as a journalist so that I can find out about things. Right now, I'm investigating people in the Congo who illegally trade wild animals. My job is to collect as much accurate information as I can and give that information to the local police. I love it, but it's a hard job. It's essential that the criminals don't figure out who I am. I find that it's hard because my life might be in danger. I have the feeling that other people would hate this job. As for me, I think it's very exciting. In my opinion, it's the most amazing job in the world.

B Underline four examples in A where the writer gives her opinion.

C Choose another news career from this lesson. Write about 100 words on whether you think you would like the job. Use the phrases from B to give opinions.

SPEAKING

A IN PAIRS **Choose a news career from this lesson. Decide what skills and experience a person needs to do this job. Write five questions that an interviewer would ask someone who was applying for the job.**

B IN PAIRS **Role-play an interview for the job. Change roles after two or three minutes. Use the Confident Communicator box to help you.**

A: So, why do you think you would make a good reporter?
B: Well, I'm very interested in current affairs and …

C IN GROUPS **Talk about how the interview went and who you think did well in the interview.**

CONFIDENT COMMUNICATOR
KEEP TALKING

To introduce important skills and experience that an interviewer hasn't asked about, use the following phrases:
Did I mention that I have experience in / know how to …?
Although I don't have much experience in …, I'm very good at …
I think my experience in … could help in my role as a/an …

Language and Life

Problem Solving – Local News

A IN PAIRS Discuss the questions.

1 Do you ever read a local newspaper (in print or online)?
2 If not, how do you get information about what's happening in your local area?
3 Do you think local newspapers are important? Why or why not?

B 9.07 Read the article about a new local newspaper. Then answer the questions.

No Story Is Too Small

With the rise of social media and online news sites, local newspapers have had a hard time. However, in a group of small towns in the Midwestern United States, print news is fighting back. Gene Nightingale and Matt Emerson, two journalists who were worried about local journalism, decided to start up their own micro newspaper. The newspaper goes on sale once a month and sells around 4,000 copies.

The newspaper is based on the idea that "no story is too small" because they write about small stories, such as how a farmer's field was flooded with water after a pipe burst, and how a new sandbox has been installed in a children's play area.

But it is these "small stories" that are the building blocks for any community. If people are aware of what is happening in their local area, they feel more connected to their community. This connection helps to create strong relationships between people who live in villages, towns, or cities. Whether it is good news, such as a local student winning a national debating competition, or bad news, such as the closure of the town library, the point is that it is news—it is something to discuss and debate and bring people together. Gene and Matt's newspaper provides that essential link.

Local newspapers are in danger. A recent report by the US Bureau of Labor Statistics found that the number of newspaper jobs fell from 458,000 in 1990 (considered to be the start of the internet age) to about 183,000 in 2016. That's a fall of almost 60%. This has an effect on local newspapers in that local news stories are not investigated in the same way. "People depend on Facebook and social media, so what's going on close to home can be ignored by larger newspapers," says Emerson. Local businesses have been very helpful and paid for the first copy of the newspaper. Nightingale and Emerson hope there might be the chance to start up other "micro newspapers" in other small towns over the next few years.

Burst pipe floods local field

Jenny McGill's winning argument

Town library in danger of closing

Read more

1 How often is the paper published? ______
2 What idea is the newspaper based on? ______
3 How many people were working in newspaper jobs in 2016? ______
4 Who helped to pay for the first copies of the newspaper? ______

C **IN PAIRS** Imagine that you work for a local daily newspaper that has lost sales. Your boss has some suggestions on how to improve sales. Choose the five best suggestions and write them in note form in the first column of the table.

My tips for improving business

1 *Include more human-interest stories and more photos.*
2 *Encourage citizen journalism where local people write stories that are important to them.*
3 *Include live-blogging on the website to cover breaking news stories. Readers can add audio and video posts.*
4 *Make online stories more personal. Allow readers to choose the news and the area that they are interested in. They receive notifications when news that's important to them happens.*
5 *Have an online-only news service. Readers join and pay a monthly fee as they would with Spotify or Netflix.*
6 *Offer reader discounts at other local businesses, e.g. a discount on a Valentine's Day meal in a local restaurant if you buy the newspaper every day for a week, for example.*
7 *Go from being a daily newspaper to a weekly newspaper.*
8 *Increase the price of the newspaper.*

	Suggestions	Advantages	Disadvantages
1			
2			
3			
4			
5			

D **IN PAIRS** Discuss the advantages and disadvantages of each of your choices. Write them in the table.

A: One advantage of using citizen journalists is that they do it for free. We can save money.

B: Yes, that's true, but they might not be very good at writing news stories.

E Compare your ideas and agree on the best five. Make some other suggestions for ways to improve sales.

F Discuss the questions.

1 Why is it useful to identify the advantages and disadvantages of a solution?
2 What other approaches to solving problems can you think of?

MAKE IT DIGITAL

Go online and find a local news website. Share some examples of interesting or amusing local news with the class.

VOCABULARY review

SCORE: / 10

A Complete the sentences with the correct words. The first letter is given.

1 Right now, I'm working as a s____________ on the magazine *Soccer Special Weekly*.
2 Your facts must be accurate, or your readers won't t____________ you to tell the truth.
3 Whenever there is b____________ around the world, I get an update on my newsfeed.
4 This is a great picture for our article, but will people be able to f____________ what it is?
5 I read the news online, but I'm not interested in h____________ stories about people I don't know.
6 In some countries, the g____________ controls the media, especially television and newspapers.
7 One of the e____________ of online news is that newspaper sales have fallen.
8 Do you speak Spanish, or would you like a t____________ to help you?
9 As an investigative journalist, my job is to try to p____________ that the story I'm investigating is true.
10 Have you seen today's h____________? They've found water on Mars!

GRAMMAR review

SCORE: / 10

A Choose the correct words.

My hero is Nellie Bly. She was **1** so / such an amazing woman. She became one of the world's first investigative journalists, writing articles about female factory workers. Male readers were **2** enough / so shocked to learn that the writer was a woman that Nellie was moved to the women's section of the paper. Nellie thought that writing about fashion and gardening wasn't **3** interesting enough / enough interesting for her. In 1888, her editor suggested she travel around the world in 80 days—something that people thought was **4** such / too dangerous for a woman to attempt. It is **5** so / such amazing that she returned in just 72 days!

B Complete the sentences with the correct modals of deduction.

1 I can't open my email. There ____________ be a problem with my wi-fi.
2 The news report says it's cold, but it ____________ be snowing. It almost never snows in Los Angeles!
3 My phone shows I have one missed call. ____________ it be about the reporter's job I applied for?
4 That newspaper ____________ be mine. My copy is in my briefcase.
5 I'm sure I know that woman. I think she ____________ be the news anchor on our local news channel.

16–20 correct: You can talk about news stories and news careers. You can use *so*, *such*, *too*, and *enough* and modals of deduction.
0–15 correct: Look again at the Vocabulary and Grammar sections in the unit.

TOTAL SCORE: / 20

WHAT DO YOU KNOW NOW? Look back at page 87 and add the words you know now to the box.

STUDY SKILLS MAKING NOTES

Take the quiz about making notes. Go to **Study Skills** on page 135 to find the answers. Then learn more about making notes.

1 When taking notes from a book, it's a good idea to write down every word you read without changing anything.
a True **b** False

2 What is plagiarism?
a writing so fast that you can't read what your notes say
b including someone else's ideas in your essay without mentioning the source

3 You can use your own symbols and abbreviations in both your notes and assignments.
a True **b** False

4 How many sets of notes should you aim to have?
a one **b** two **c** three

UNIT

10 Got It?

WHAT DO YOU ALREADY KNOW?

1 Think about the things you are good at in different areas of your life. Write the things.

2 IN PAIRS Share and compare your ideas. Add more words to your lists.

At home

At school or work

Sports and art

VIDEO

DISCUSS & SHARE

3 IN GROUPS Watch the video and answer the question.

SYM Would you use your talent to express your creativity or make money?

In this unit, you will ...

- talk about your talents and abilities, ask and answer questions for a talent show audition, and share advice on how to succeed in the music industry.
- use thinking skills: question, analyze, and evaluate.
- read about what causes talent.
- use strategies and language to talk about your achievements politely, control your nerves when speaking to a group, and use idioms in informal contexts.
- use communication skills to make judgments and choose winners of a talent contest.
- follow a talent scout to learn about this job and the skills needed to be in this industry.

READING

A **Think about different kinds of great artists. What talents do they have?**

B 10.01 **Read the text. Then choose what type of writing you think it is.**

a a blog entry **b** a newspaper article **c** a popular science magazine article

Ask an Expert

Petra Waterhouse from Berlin asks: Are great artists born or made? In other words, is **talent** genetic or is it learned?

Professor Anna Felix answers: 1 I think the short answer is both. Musical ability is a good example here because some people are born with greater **potential** than others, but without hard work and practice, they don't achieve it. **2** A study of 1,211 sets of **identical twins** born between 1959 and 1985 found that even when one twin practiced music regularly and one didn't, it made no difference. In one case, one man practiced for over 20,000 hours more than his twin, but their musical ability was about the same. This goes some way to showing us that at least some talents are genetic. **3** I believe they are part of our DNA and we probably inherit them from our parents. So, thank you, Mom and Dad!

4 A different study by Professor Zach Hambrick investigated 14 studies of top chess players and musicians: could their level of ability be explained by their hours of practice? The answer was "no." **5** Practice only made about a 30% difference to how good these people were. In previous research, Hambrick argues that what is important is the ability to remember things. Having an excellent **memory** can mean the difference between just being smart and being a genius.

6 One **theory** is that it takes 10,000 hours of practice to become an expert at something. There is possibly a degree of truth in this (although this will probably depend on what you are practicing). But if your DNA gives you a love of chess, languages, music, or soccer, I'd **assume** that would make you more likely to be prepared to put in those long hours of practice anyway.

GLOSSARY

genetic (adj): related to chemicals in a cell that are passed from one generation to another
inherit (v): get something (e.g., a talent, a medical condition) from one's parents
genius (n): a very intelligent person

C **READING SKILL—Recognize fact and opinion** **Read the text in READING B again. Are the underlined sentences (1–6) facts or opinions? Write *F* (fact) or *O* (opinion).**

1 ____ 2 ____ 3 ____ 4 ____ 5 ____ 6 ____

D **THINKING SKILL—Question** **Do you think great artists are born or made? What has helped the artists you know become famous?**

VOCABULARY

A **Match the words with their definitions.**

1 assume (v): ____
2 potential (n): ____
3 memory (n): ____
4 talent (n): ____
5 identical twins (n): ____
6 theory (n): ____

a brothers or sisters born at the same time that look exactly the same
b an idea that explains how something happens
c the ability to remember things
d a natural ability for something
e an ability that may be developed in the future
f believe that something is true without proof

MAKE IT DIGITAL

Go online to find profiles of talented people. Make a note of the adjectives that are used to describe them.

GRAMMAR reported speech: statements

A We use reported speech to report something a person has said or written. Read the example from READING B. How does the tense change between direct speech and reported speech?

"I think the short answer is both." (direct speech)
She said she thought the short answer was both. (reported speech)

1 ______________________________

B Complete the table.

Tense	Tense Change	Direct Speech	Reported Speech (note reporting verb)
simple present	simple past	"Jack is very talented."	She **said** (that) Jack was very talented.
present progressive	**1** __________	"I'm learning the saxophone."	She **told me** (that) she was learning the saxophone.
present perfect	past perfect	"I have never seen *The X Factor.*"	She **admitted** (that) she **2** __________ *The X Factor.*
simple past	past perfect	**3** "My dad __________ good at singing."	She **explained** (that) her dad had been good at singing.
future with *will*	*will* becomes **4** __________	"Macy will be a genius one day."	She **mentioned** (that) Macy would be a genius one day.

C Choose the correct options for the rules.

1 Use quotation marks for **direct speech** / **reported speech**.
2 In reported speech, the verb tense in the noun clause changes to the **past** / **future** form.

For more practice, go to page 155.

D Rewrite the statements in your notebooks using reported speech.

1 "Lyndon is a very talented soccer player." (the coach, say)
2 "I don't really like abstract art." (Alessandro, admit)
3 "We will practice the dance routine this weekend." (the class, promise)
4 "I learned how to draw by watching video clips online." (Alicia, tell me)

SPEAKING

A Think about something that you have learned to do well. Make notes.

- what you learned
- how you learned it
- how you felt about it

B IN PAIRS Take turns talking about the thing you learned in A. Ask and answer questions to find out more. Use the Confident Communicator box to help you.

C IN PAIRS Now work in a different pair. Report what your first partner told you.

Nina said she had learned to windsurf when she was 15 …,

CONFIDENT COMMUNICATOR
KEEP TALKING

To talk about your own achievements without sounding overconfident, use the following phrases:
It took a lot of hard work, but I managed to learn …
I was really lucky, because I found it easy to …
I had a really good teacher/tutor/friend who helped me to …

LESSON 2 TV Talent Shows

LISTENING

A **Which TV talent shows are popular in your country? Do you like watching them? Why or why not?**

B **10.02 Listen to short excerpts from a TV talent show. Match the speakers (1–3) with their acts (a–d). There's one act you don't need.**

1 Noel ____	**a** a ventriloquist
2 Caitlyn ____	**b** a magician
3 Bobby ____	**c** a comedian
	d a singer

GLOSSARY

audition (n): a short performance so someone can decide if you are good enough to perform at an event

C **10.03 LISTENING SKILL—Identify attitude Listen to the same speakers talking about their experience after the TV talent show auditions. Choose how they think they did.**

1 Noel
a very well **b** OK **c** badly

2 Caitlyn
a very well **b** OK **c** badly

3 Bobby
a very well **b** OK **c** badly

MAKE IT REAL

If you don't do something you were planning to do because you're too nervous or scared, you can use the phrasal verb *chicken out*.

I was supposed to go to an audition for The Big Break, but I ***chickened out*** *at the last minute.*

D **THINKING SKILL—Analyze Discuss this statement: "Only a small number of people who appear on TV talent shows are really talented." Do you agree or not?**

VOCABULARY phrasal verbs

A **Match the phrasal verbs in bold (1–5) with the definitions (a–e).**

1 Bridget's dance classes are not easy, but she plans to **keep on** going. ____
2 The director **turned down** a lot of people who auditioned for the play. ____
3 When will you **come back** from the audition? ____
4 Please **fill out** this form with your name and contact information. ____
5 Over 100 people **showed up** at the movie studio for the audition. ____

a to arrive at a place
b to return to a place
c to complete a form
d to say no to an offer or request
e to continue doing something

PRONUNCIATION stress in phrasal verbs

A **10.04 Listen to the sentences. Underline the stressed word in each one. Can you notice the difference?**

1 **a** He filled out the form.	**b** He filled it out.
2 **a** She turned down the job.	**b** She turned it down.
3 **a** I gave up dance classes.	**b** I gave them up.

GRAMMAR reported speech: questions

A Read the direct questions and reported questions from LISTENING B. Notice how the tense changes are the same as in reported statements.

1 He asked, "Do you need some water?" ⟶ He asked whether I needed some water.
2 He asked, "Are you feeling confident?" ⟶ He asked if I was feeling confident.
3 He asked, "How long have you been doing your act?" ⟶ He asked how long I'd been doing my act.
4 He asked, "Who are you?" ⟶ He asked who I was.

B Choose the correct options to complete the grammar rules.

1 Use *if* or *whether* in reported *yes/no* questions / reported information questions.
2 Use a question word in reported *yes/no* questions / reported information questions.
3 Use / Don't use auxiliary verbs in reported questions.
4 The word order in reported questions is the same as / different from word order in affirmative sentences.
5 Use / Don't use a question mark at the end of reported questions.

For more practice, go to page 156.

C Rewrite the direct questions as reported questions.

1 She asked, "Do you ever watch TV talent shows?" ⟶ She asked __________.
2 She asked, "What are you wearing to the audition?" ⟶ She asked __________.
3 She asked, "How long have you been waiting?" ⟶ She asked __________.
4 She asked, "Who is the best candidate?" ⟶ She asked __________.

D IN PAIRS Think about the last time you spoke to a close friend. What did he or she ask you about? Report it to your partner.

Last night, I spoke to my friend Estefan. He asked me if I had done anything interesting …

SPEAKING

A Imagine you are going to an audition for a TV talent show.

Would you …

- sing a song?
- dance?
- do something else?
- tell jokes?
- do a magic trick?

B Write questions that an interviewer might ask you at the audition.

C IN PAIRS Ask and answer the questions from B.

A: Have you been in any other talent shows?
B: No, this is the first time I've auditioned.
A: And how long have you been doing magic?
B: I've been doing magic since I was six.

D IN GROUPS Report what your partner told you using reported speech. Use the Confident Communicator box to help you.

CONFIDENT COMMUNICATOR
KEEP TALKING

You might feel nervous talking to a large group of people or the whole class. To help in these situations, you can try the following things:

- Control your breathing; breathe in and out slowly before you begin.
- Focus on what you are saying and not on your audience.
- Speak slowly.

VOCABULARY idioms and sayings connected to success

A Match the idioms (1–6) with the meanings (a–f). Use a dictionary or look online if you need help.

1 be in the right place at the right time ____
2 it isn't what you know; it's who you know ____
3 set your sights on something ____
4 have your heart set on something ____
5 dream big ____
6 be hungry for success ____

a focus on something as your goal
b want something very much
c be lucky because of where you are and when
d make progress in life because of personal connections
e have goals or hopes that are difficult to achieve
f want to do very well

B IN PAIRS Do you know any other idioms about success in English or another language? What are they?

LISTENING

A What special talents or abilities do you think you need to succeed in the music industry?

B 10.05 Listen to this radio call-in show. What does Elsa Hardman do?

a She runs a music website.
b She manages a music store.
c She owns a record company.

C 10.05 LISTENING SKILL—Listen to take notes Listen again and complete the notes. Remember that you don't need to write every word you hear.

Tips to Make It in the Music Industry!

Starting a Record Company:

- *Dream big!*
- *Go out and* **1** ____________
- *Ask people with more experience for* **2** ____________

Finding Work as a Singer:

- *Keep goals* **3** ____________
- *Sing at a local show*
- *Think of yourself as a* **4** ____________
- *Be* **5** ____________

D THINKING SKILL—Evaluate How do people measure success in your country? Discuss the top three things that you think make a person successful.

A: I think the three things that make someone successful are hard work, talent and the people you know.
B: What about luck? You need to be lucky too!
A: But is luck more important than hard work?

WRITING

A Read the informal email. Match the items (a–e) with the underlined parts of the email (1–5).

a informal greeting ____
b informal closing ____
c contraction ____
d informal punctuation ____
e signature ____

New Message

From: Delia Roberts — Cc Bcc

To: Henri Martinez

[1] Hi Henri,

I hope [2] you're well. I'm writing to ask a favor. A friend has her heart set on working in the music industry. She's a fantastic singer, but she isn't very confident. I thought since you're a music producer you'd have some advice I can give her before she gives up. Any information welcome [3]!

[4] Thanks for your help!

[5] Delia

Send

B Now read Henri's reply. How is the style of Henri's email different from the email in A?

New Message

From: Henri Martinez — Cc Bcc

To: Delia Roberts

Dear Delia,

Thank you for your email. I am pleased to hear that you are well. I have some advice for your friend. She will need to make a recording of her voice and send it to as many producers as possible. We are always looking for new talent, so send it to me, too. We will be able to decide if she has real musical talent.

Yours sincerely,

Henri Martinez

Send

C Rewrite Henri's email giving advice to Delia, but in a more informal style. Use the points in A.

SPEAKING

A IN PAIRS Read the emails you rewrote. Whose email sounded more informal?

B IN GROUPS Report the advice from your partner's email for making it in the music industry. Ask the group: whose advice is the most useful?

A: Jose said that she should use social media to advertise her talents.

B: And Francesca said she should practice at home to improve her confidence.

C IN GROUPS Discuss the statement. Use the Confident Communicator box to help you.

It isn't what you know, but who you know that matters in the music industry.

CONFIDENT COMMUNICATOR
KEEP TALKING

Use only a few, well-known idioms in your informal speaking and writing.
Make sure that you know the meaning of an idiom before you use it.

Language and Life

Communication – Talent Contest

A **Have you or anyone you know ever taken part in a talent contest? What was the experience like?**

B **10.06 Read the article about the beginnings of TV talent shows. Then answer the questions.**

Talent Contests

A TV talent show audition

The TV talent show *Got Talent*, started by Simon Cowell in 2004, has become a global success story. Viewers watch the shows in 58 countries. In 2014, *Guinness World Records* named it the most successful reality TV show ever. A number of other audition-based shows, such as *The Voice* and *The X Factor*, are also popular with audiences across the planet. And the reason? People love watching as the contestants go from nothing to huge success over a few weeks and months. But how did it all start?

Back in 1934, a radio show called *Original Amateur Hour* began in the US. After some success, it moved to TV in 1948. That show was similar to talent shows today. TV professionals traveled the country looking for entertainers who then went to New York for the auditions. The entertainers would audition for the judges on TV, and if chosen, they would come back and audition again. The audience would vote for their favorite act by phone or by mail. The final competition was at Madison Square Garden and the winners received a trophy and $1,500.

Original Amateur Hour helped to create a number of stars. Frank Sinatra performed on the radio show. Surprisingly, Elvis Presley wasn't successful when he auditioned for the show in Tupelo, Mississippi.

Another talent competition was *Star Search*. *Star Search* was different because entertainers competed in different categories, such as best male singer and best female singer. The prize money was $100,000 for each category. Many well-known pop stars and singing groups auditioned when they were younger, including Justin Timberlake, Destiny's Child, Christina Aguilera, Britney Spears, and Usher.

American Idol started on TV in 2002. Many more TV talent shows followed: *So You Think You Can Dance*, *The X Factor*, *Rockstar INXS*, *The Sing-Off*, *Dancing With the Stars*, and most recently, *The Voice*. Past winners of *Got Talent* include a performing police dog team, acrobats, ventriloquists, wheelchair dancers, and even Rubik's cube puzzle solvers.

1 What did the winners of *Original Amateur Hour* win? ______
2 Who auditioned, but did not get a place, on *Original Amateur Hour*? ______
3 What was different about the format of *Star Search*? ______
4 When did *American Idol* first appear on TV? ______
5 What talents do the past winners of *Got Talent* have? ______
6 Why might these talents be interesting to watch on TV? ______

C **IN PAIRS Talk to your partner and discuss what talents you have.**

A: I have a cool talent. I can play music using glasses of water!
B: Really? That's amazing. I can play guitar.
A: Maybe we could perform together!

D Your class is going to hold a talent contest. Choose three classmates to perform. Decide if you want to be a contestant or a judge and follow the instructions.

Contestants: Get into groups. Explain what you want to do. Choose from one of the following:

- singing
- dancing
- playing an instrument
- reading a poem out loud
- acting out a scene from a movie or theater show
- another talent

Think about the questions you may be asked in the audition and work together to prepare clear and precise answers.

Possible Questions	Possible Answers
I think they might ask me how long I have been playing piano.	*I've been playing piano for five years.*

Judges: Get into groups. Discuss and agree how you are going to give scores for each contestant. Are you going to judge them on:

- talent?
- effort?
- appearance?
- a combination of these things?

Think about what you want to ask in the audition and work together to prepare clear questions.

Possible Questions
I'd like to ask why they want to be in the talent contest.

E IN PAIRS Find a partner from the opposite group (contestants or judges). Report the questions that your group prepared and make sure they are the same.

A: Our group thought you would ask us how long we had been playing an instrument

B: Our group had that question. We also decided to ask you why you wanted to be in the talent contest.

F Return to your groups. Record your questions then hold the talent contest.

Contestants: Perform in front of the judges. Answer any questions as clearly as possible.
Judges: Ask questions that you made a note of.

G Decide on the winner(s) as a class. Explain what you liked about each performance and why.

H Discuss the questions.

1. Were you happy with your questions and answers? Did they help you to communicate clearly?
2. In what other situations might you have to plan questions to ask someone or plan answers to give to someone?
3. What other factors contribute to effective communication?

MAKE IT DIGITAL

Record the talent contest. Decide whose performance was the best. Who definitely has talent?

VOCABULARY review

SCORE: / 10

A Complete the sentences with the idioms from the box.

dream big | hungry for success | in the right place | set his heart on | set his sights on

1 Eliza works hard because she is ______________________.
2 Be sure to ______________________! Then you will have a goal to work toward.
3 Nat has ______________________ a singing career. He even has a manager!
4 I was ______________________ at the right time, and I got a record deal while I was at music school.
5 Sam has ______________________ being a rock star when he leaves school!

B Complete the sentences with a phrasal verb from the box that means the same as the verb in parentheses.

come back | fill out | keep on going | make up | show up

1 If you forget the dance steps in the show, ______________ (invent) your own steps.
2 The theater doors don't open until 8 p.m., so you should ______________ (return) then.
3 To enter the talent show, you need to ______________ (complete) an application form.
4 If you've failed your music exam five times, ______________ (continue) until you pass!
5 Auditions for the talent show start at 10 a.m., so please ______________ (arrive) just before then.

GRAMMAR review

SCORE: / 10

A Rewrite the numbered sentences in your notebook as reported speech. Use the verbs in parentheses.

Kyle: **1** I'm doing a project about unusual talents (tell). **2** Do you know anyone who has one? (ask)
Dan: **3** My cousin Elena has a cool talent. (say)
Kyle: **4** What can she do? (want to know)
Dan: **5** She can juggle. (explain)
Kyle: **6** Where did she learn to do that? (ask)
Dan: **7** She took a circus class. (say) **8** Have you ever taken a circus class? (ask)
Kyle: **9** I'm not good at that kind of thing! (admit)
Dan: **10** Most people aren't. (say)

16–20 correct: You can talk about your talents and abilities and use phrasal verbs and idioms connected to success. You can use reported statements and questions.
0–15 correct: Look again at the Vocabulary and Grammar sections in the unit.

TOTAL SCORE: / 20

WHAT DO YOU KNOW NOW? Look back at page 97 and add the words you know now to the boxes.

FOLLOW A PRO ENTERTAINMENT

Take the quiz about entertainment. Go to Follow A Pro on page 136 to find the answers. Then read about the entertainment industry.

1 Which country has the most televisions, with approximately 400 million?
a Russia **b** China **c** the US

2 In what year was the first in-flight movie shown?
a 1925 **b** 1945 **c** 1965

3 Which Hollywood actor was first spotted by a talent scout having an argument in a bank?
a Jennifer Lawrence **b** Natalie Portman **c** Charlize Theron

4 How many boys auditioned for the leading role in the first Harry Potter movie?
a 160 **b** 1,600 **c** 16,000

UNIT 11

Money in the Bank

WHAT DO YOU ALREADY KNOW?

1 **Think about words you know related to money and finances. Write the words.**

2 **IN PAIRS** **Share and compare your ideas. Add more words to your lists.**

Money/Finances

VIDEO

DISCUSS & SHARE

3 **IN GROUPS** **Watch the video and answer the question.**

SYM Is it better to save for the future or enjoy your money now?

In this unit, you will ...

- discuss who you would employ if you were a millionaire, share ideas about what to do with a fortune, and compare your budget with that of a partner.
- use thinking skills: question, apply, and recall.
- read about the gig economy.
- use strategies and language to talk about imagined future situations, collaborate on creative ideas, and politely refuse to answer a question.
- use collaboration skills to manage a budget.
- learn tips for personal development.

READING

A **Do you know what the "gig economy" is? Can you figure out what it is from the pictures?**

B **11.01 READING SKILL—Read for the main idea** **Read the job ad, article, and business profile. Match a title with each one.**

a Every Day is Different! **b** Calling All Computer Game Fans … **c** Changes to Our Working and Home Lives

1 _____ We're **hiring** in your area! Would you like to earn some extra cash? Are you happy to do freelance work from home? If the answer is "yes," then give Reviews4U a call at 800-555-3210. We're a software company that needs gamers to test our new range of exciting PC games. We'll pay $40 for each gaming review you send to us. No **contract**, no stress, and hours that work for you.

2 _____ Today's workers no longer expect to have the same job for life. The gig economy means that more and more people are working for themselves, offering their services and time **in exchange for** cash, but with no contract, no **pension**, and no vacation or sick pay. The way we take care of chores has changed at home, too. We have people take care of our gardens and yards, we make someone else walk our dogs because we're too busy to do it ourselves, and we get people to decorate our apartments. We have our groceries delivered and we get our houses cleaned. Interestingly, there are things that we used to get *others* to do in the past that we now do *ourselves* because of changes in technology. Now, we book our own flights online instead of getting a travel agent to do it for us. We also manage our own money online without the help of a bank clerk.

GigGetters

3 _____ CeeCee Rogers, a tech worker in New York City, was **laid off** in 2018. She knew it might take a long time to find another job in her field.

"I wasn't sure what to do," explains CeeCee. "When I lost my job, it was a big shock. Luckily, I found out about GigGetters and I signed up with them. They have me do various gigs so I can make money while I'm looking for a more **permanent** job. I enjoy it. No day is the same!"

C **Read the texts again. Write *True* or *False*.**

1 The job at Reviews4U pays the same amount of money every month. _____
2 Working for Reviews4U would mean working in an office. _____
3 Text 2 includes information about disadvantages for workers in a gig economy. _____
4 CeeCee wants to work for GigGetters for as long as possible. _____

GLOSSARY

freelance (adj): not employed by a particular company, but working for them on a temporary basis

D **THINKING SKILL—Question** **What are the advantages of gig work? What are the disadvantages?**

VOCABULARY

A Complete the sentences with a word or phrase in bold in READING B.

1. My friend gave me a skirt that didn't fit her ______________ a brown jacket that I never wear.
2. I was ______________ a month ago, so I'm looking for another job.
3. When people retire from work, they usually get a regular amount of money called a ______________ from the company or government.
4. Did you sign a ______________ with your company when you started?
5. Dave has a temporary job, but he's looking for something ______________.
6. This restaurant is ______________ chefs and servers.

MAKE IT YOURS

Go online or use a dictionary to find job advertisements in English for your chosen career. Are most companies hiring permanent workers, temporary workers, or gig workers?

GRAMMAR causatives with *have, get,* and *make*

A Underline examples in Text 2 in READING B of things we pay people to do for us and things we do ourselves.

B Complete the grammar rules with forms from the box.

base form of verb (x 2) infinitive past participle

1. Use *have* or *get* to talk about paying or asking someone to do something for you.
   subject + *have/get* + object + ______________ → I have/get my house cleaned.
2. Use *make* when you force or persuade someone to do something.
   subject + *make* + object + ______________ → I made my brother clean his room.
3. Use *have someone do something* to talk about someone who does a job for you.
   subject + *have* + person + ______________ → We had a mechanic fix the car.
4. Use *get someone to do something* when you ask, persuade, or pay someone to do something for you.
   subject + *get* + person + ______________ → They got a vet to check their dog's health.

For more practice, go to page 156.

C Complete the sentences with the correct forms of the words in parentheses.

If you think being one of the world's wealthiest people sounds like fun, think about all the staff you'd need to hire just to keep your life in order! You'd need **1** ______________ (get / housekeeper / clean) the house. You'd have to **2** ______________ (have / nanny / take care of) your children and a private tutor **3** ______________ (make / them / do) their homework. But think of the advantages! When you came home at the end of a long day, you could **4** ______________ (have / your meal / cook) by your personal chef and **5** ______________ (make / butler / bring) your slippers for you before you put your feet up in front of the TV!

D IN PAIRS Talk about things you have, get, or make other people do for you.

SPEAKING

A You have an unlimited amount of money. Make notes about what you would get these people to do for you.

- a hairdresser
- a mechanic
- a chef
- a dog walker

B IN PAIRS Talk about your ideas. Use the Confident Communicator box to help you.

C IN GROUPS What jobs would you like to have people do for you and what jobs you would prefer to do yourself?

CONFIDENT COMMUNICATOR
START TALKING

To start a conversation about things you dream of for the future, use:
You know what I'd do if I were ...?
You know what I'd do if I had enough money? I'd have a chef cook all my meals.

LESSON 2 Giving Away Money

VOCABULARY money verbs and nouns

A Read the definitions. Write the related nouns. Use a dictionary if needed.

Verb	Noun (thing)	Noun (person)
donate: to give something such as money to a charity	**1** ____________: an amount of something such as money given to a charity	**2** ____________: a person who donates something
contribute: to give something such as money to help achieve something	**3** ____________: a gift or payment you make to help achieve something	**4** ____________: a person who contributes something

B IN GROUPS Do you know individuals who have donated large sums of money to a particular cause in your country or abroad? Discuss.

Examples: George Soros Bill and Melinda Gates Oprah Winfrey Alcario and Carmen Castellano

LISTENING

A IN PAIRS Do you ever donate money to charity? What kind of charities do you support?

1

animal charities

2
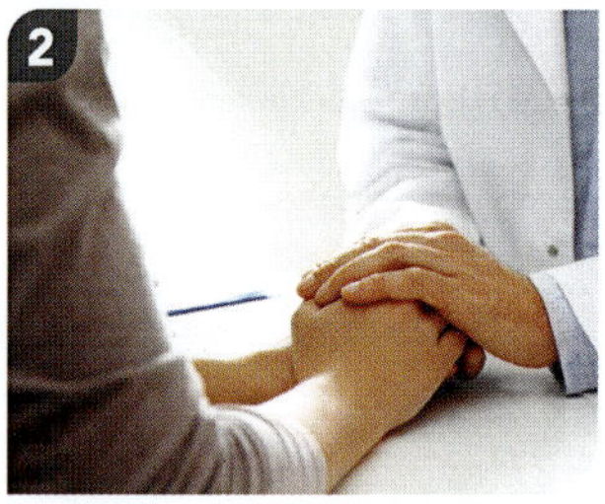
charities that help people with health problems

3

educational charities

4

environmental charities

5

charities that provide food, water, or housing

B 11.02 LISTENING SKILL—Listen for specific information Listen to an interview. Then complete the sentences.

1 The interviewer says that George Soros has donated over ____________ billion dollars to charity.
2 The charity called *Rainbows* helps ____________.
3 Pat says that people can offer to work in the charity's thrift ____________.
4 Danny says you can do online ____________ to help charities.
5 Danny says an organization called ____________ helps people who need food.
6 Pat's charity has received ____________ thousand dollars in foreign currency collected on planes.

GLOSSARY

campaign manager (n): a person who organizes ways to make money for a charity, organization, or political party
volunteer (n): a person who is not paid for the work they do
foreign currency (n phr): money from another country

C 11.02 IN PAIRS Compare your answers. Then listen again and check.

D THINKING SKILL—Apply Is it better to donate time or money to a charity? Give reasons.

GRAMMAR verbs with gerund, infinitive, or both

A **Read the examples from LISTENING B. Notice how some verbs are followed by the infinitive (*to* + base form of verb), the gerund (verb + *–ing*), or both.**

Many people decide to give cash …
Some people prefer doing these events
Have you considered playing games online?

B **Complete the rules with one of the verbs underlined in the examples from A. Then complete the example sentences.**

1 Some verbs (such as ____________ *agree*, *want*, *offer*, etc.) are followed by infinitives.
EXAMPLE: Last year, my cousin did a 10k fun run and now, I really ____________ to do one too.

2 Some verbs (such as ____________ *suggest*, *deny*, *keep*, etc.) are followed by gerunds.
EXAMPLE: For a charity event, my friend ____________ raising money by playing games online.

3 Verbs that describe feelings (such as ____________ *dislike*, *like*, *love*, *hate*, etc.) can be followed by both gerunds and infinitives.
EXAMPLE: I could never run a marathon! I absolutely ____________ running.

For more practice, go to page 157.

C **Complete the text with the infinitive or gerund form of the verb in parentheses. If both forms are possible, write both.**

Inheriting money can be hard, especially when the person who dies leaves instructions about what the person must (or mustn't) agree **1** ____________________ (do) to get the money. Leona Helmsley, a hotel owner, left $12 million to her dog when she died. However, she gave instructions that two of her grandchildren would only inherit money if they promised **2** ____________________ (visit) their father's grave regularly. Henry Budd of London, who died in 1862, hated **3** ____________________ (see) men with mustaches so much that he refused **4** ____________________ (leave) money to his two sons unless they avoided **5** ____________________ (grow) facial hair. It seems some people just like **6** ____________________ (give) instructions even in death!

D **IN PAIRS Complete the sentences with information that is true for you. Discuss with your partner.**

1 I dislike ____________________
2 I sometimes help ____________________
3 I avoid ____________________
4 I really love ____________________
5 I always refuse ____________________

SPEAKING

A **Imagine that you have inherited $1 million. Would you spend it, save it, or give it to charity? Make notes.**

B **IN GROUPS Share your ideas. Give specific information about what you would do with the money. Use the Confident Communicator box to help you.**

CONFIDENT COMMUNICATOR
START TALKING

When you collaborate on creative ideas, it's good to start by going around the group, giving everyone the chance to talk about their ideas without interruptions. That way, everyone in the group can express their ideas with the full attention of everyone else.

LESSON 3 Spending Money

VOCABULARY paying for things

A Label the pictures (1–6) with phrases from the box.

ATM / cash machine | cash | change | contactless payment | credit card | debit card

1 

2 

3 

4 

5 

6 

B **IN PAIRS** Talk about what you use to pay for different things.

A: I usually use cash to pay for lunch.

B: I sometimes use a debit card when I buy clothes.

PRONUNCIATION /tʃ/ versus /ʃ/

A **11.03** Listen to how these words are pronounced. Notice the difference between the /tʃ/ and /ʃ/ sounds.

<u>ch</u>ange   ca<u>sh</u> ma<u>ch</u>ine

B **11.04** Practice saying these sentences. Then listen and check.

1 Do you have any change?
2 I'm going to use the cash machine.

LISTENING

A What do you spend money on? How do you manage your money?

B **11.05 LISTENING SKILL—Listen for the main idea** Listen to a radio show. People are talking about the ways they manage their money. Match the speakers (1–4) with the ways to manage money (a–d).

1 Speaker 1 ____
2 Speaker 2 ____
3 Speaker 3 ____
4 Speaker 4 ____

a pays someone else to manage their money for them.
b says that they mostly use debit cards when they shop.
c uses traditional ways of managing their money.
d uses an app to help them manage their money.

C **11.05** Listen again and choose the correct speakers.

Which speaker …

1	isn't very good at managing money?	1	2	3	4
2	rarely uses a credit card?	1	2	3	4
3	would rather earn money than manage it?	1	2	3	4
4	likes to keep a physical record of her/his spending?	1	2	3	4
5	uses computer programs to manage her/his money?	1	2	3	4
6	uses their smartphone to manage her/his money?	1	2	3	4

MAKE IT REAL

To *splurge* means to spend a lot of money.
Maria used her birthday money to splurge on expensive new shoes.

D **IN PAIRS THINKING SKILL—Recall** Try to remember how much money you spent yesterday. What did you spend it on? How did you pay?

A: I really don't remember. I know I bought a soda and a sandwich.

B: Is that it? I'm sure you bought more than that.

WRITING

A **A friend is visiting you from abroad. Read her email. What does she need advice about?**

1 restaurants **2** sightseeing **3** money

New Message

How are you doing? I'm really excited about seeing you in a few weeks. Can you give me some advice?

- Should I bring cash with me? If so, how much do you think I'll need per day for food, shopping, sightseeing?
- Should I change my dollars into the local currency here or wait until I'm there?
- Can I use my debit card or credit card at the ATMs?
- Please let me know what you think is best. A list of do's and don'ts would be great.

See you soon!
Amelia

Send

B **Think about Amelia's questions. Add advice to the table.**

Do's	Don'ts
change some money before you arrive	bring too much cash

C **Write an email to Amelia. Include the information from your table in B.**

D IN PAIRS **Share your emails. Did your partner answer all of Amelia's questions?**

SPEAKING

A **Find out what the average income is for people in your country per month. Write it in the table. Then fill in the amounts of money you think you would need to spend per month on these things.**

Item	Amount	Item	Amount	Item	Amount
rent/mortgage	**1**	food	**2**	clothes	**3**
entertainment/going out	**4**	travel/transportation	**5**	phone	**6**
household bills (water, gas, electricity, etc.)	**7**	other	**8**		

1 Total monthly income: ____________ **2** Total monthly spending: ____________

B IN PAIRS **Compare the amount of money you imagine you would spend on each thing.**

A: I think I would spend about $100 a month on food.

B: Really? I think I'd need to spend more than that. I wrote $150.

C IN GROUPS **Report to the group what you have learned about your partner's budget. What advice would you give to people who have spent too much? Use the Confident Communicator box to help you.**

Rico enjoys eating out. He thinks he'd spend between $60 and $100 a month. Maybe he should eat out less.

CONFIDENT COMMUNICATOR

KEEP TALKING

Money can be a hard topic to talk about. There are phrases you can use to refuse, politely, to answer questions you aren't comfortable with:
I'd rather not answer that question, if you don't mind.
That's a personal question. I'd rather not say.
I'm sorry, but that isn't information I want to share.

Language and Life

Collaborate – A Budget

A **Are there any businesses near you that were set up by local people? What kinds of things do they sell? Are they popular?**

B **11.06 Read the newspaper article about two friends who set up a business. Answer the questions.**

Business Profile: KylieBelle's Bakery

Meet Annabelle Eggers and Kylie Howell, a pair of high school friends who recently set up KylieBelle's Bakery, a bakery and coffee shop on the North Shore. The pair both left successful careers in law to start their own business. But things didn't get off to a good start.

"It hasn't been easy," Kylie explains, when we meet up at the bakery on a Sunday morning. "I don't think we realized how much hard work it would be. We thought we'd be doing the jobs we love all day, which for us is making cakes and serving customers. But actually, there's a lot more involved, like accounting. Also, we had an awful first day." The pair had to close the bakery after a serious fire in their kitchen on the day they opened. "It was terrible," admits Annabelle. "We thought we might not be able to afford to open again after the accident. We were both in tears."

Luckily, a local resident, Marlene Parks, offered to help by investing over $10,000 in the business. "I was looking for a small business to invest some money in," says Marlene. "And who doesn't love a nice bakery in their local area? I hope the business does really well and I wish Annabelle and Kylie lots of luck." The women used the money to get builders to repair the kitchen, and the bakery reopened two weeks later.

"Thanks to Marlene, we were able to get the business open again. We need to pay her back, obviously, but it meant we could start making money. The business is doing really well. We're going to have a new seating area built outside so we can serve more of our cakes. People love our white chocolate cheesecake!"

1. What profession did Annabelle and Kylie use to work in? ______________________
2. What happened on the first day the bakery opened? ______________________
3. How did the women get money for builders to repair the kitchen? ______________________
4. What are they planning to build outside and why? ______________________

C IN PAIRS Imagine you want to open a small business in your city or town with your partner. You have a budget of $10,000 to get the business started. Together, discuss the questions and reach an agreement for each point.

1 What kind of small business will you open?
2 Where will it be located?
3 What is the rent?
4 What will you call it?
5 What product or service will you sell?
6 How much will the product or service cost?
7 What kinds of payment will you accept (cash, credit cards, debit cards)?
8 What kinds of problems do you think the business might have?
9 What can you do about these problems?

D IN PAIRS Before you open the business, you need to decide which jobs you can do yourself and which you are going to get someone else to do for you. Decide together and write the jobs and the costs in the correct column.

Jobs we can do ourselves	Jobs we need to get someone else to do	Expected costs for jobs other people will do
delivering leaflets	*installing new kitchen equipment*	

E Underline the jobs in D that will cost a lot to have someone else do. Could you do any of them yourself? Negotiate with each other to decide who could do which job.

F IN GROUPS Share your ideas. Find out which businesses are within the $10,000 budget.

G Discuss the questions.

1 Did you and your partner work well together? How did you overcome any disagreements?
2 In what other situations might you have to collaborate and agree on a solution?

MAKE IT DIGITAL

Find and read an online article about starting a new business. What other things should you consider that were not discussed in this lesson?

VOCABULARY review

SCORE: / 10

A Complete the sentences with words from the box.

contract contribution donor pension permanent

1 In some countries, you can receive a ________________ from the government at the age of 60.
2 Did you sign a ________________ when you started your new job?
3 This is a ________________ job, so you'll have a fixed schedule.
4 A generous celebrity ________________ has given $1 million to this charity.
5 Did you make a ________________ to any charities last year?

B Choose the five correct answers to complete the sentences.

1 I don't like borrowing money, so I don't have any **credit** / **debit** cards.
2 Do you have any **ATMs** / **cash**? This machine doesn't accept **change** / **contactless** payments.
3 The **credit card** / **ATM** isn't working so I haven't got any **cash** / **cash machines** at all.

GRAMMAR review

SCORE: / 10

A Choose the correct words.

1 She is **having** / **making** her hair cut at the hairdresser at the moment.
2 Did you **have** / **get** a mechanic fix your car?
3 They are **getting** / **making** a painter to decorate their new bathroom.
4 Mom **made** / **got** the kids mow the lawn before they had lunch.
5 Will he **get** / **have** a taxi to take him to the airport at 3 a.m.?

B Complete the sentences with the correct forms of the verbs in parentheses. Write both forms where possible.

1 My manager has agreed ________________ (give) me time off when I move.
2 I've decided ________________ (save) some money every month for a vacation.
3 Marcus promised ________________ (not/spend) a lot of money on his fiancée's Christmas gifts.
4 I prefer ________________ (pay) for things with my debit card rather than with a credit card.
5 I avoid ________________ (waste) money buying things I don't need.

16–20 correct: You can talk about money and paying for things. You can use *have, make* and *get* and verbs with the gerund, infinitive, or both.
0–15 correct: Look again at the Vocabulary and Grammar sections in the unit.

TOTAL SCORE: / 20

WHAT DO YOU KNOW NOW? Look back at page 107 and add the words you know now to the box.

STUDY SKILLS PERSONAL DEVELOPMENT

Take the quiz about personal development. Go to **Study Skills** on page 137 to find the answers. Then learn more about personal development.

1 Recording yourself answering questions is a useful study technique.
a True **b** False

2 Studying for short periods of time is not effective.
a True **b** False

3 What is overlearning?
a It's when you work too hard and get very tired.
b It's when you go over to a friend's house to study.
c It's when you continue learning something even when you think you've already learned it.

4 What percentage of students admit to studying for exams at the very last minute?
a 99% **b** 90% **c** 65% **d** 51%

UNIT 12 Inside Advertising

WHAT DO YOU ALREADY KNOW?

1 Think about ads you like. Write words to describe them.

2 **IN PAIRS** Share and compare your ideas. Add more words to your lists.

Ads:

VIDEO

DISCUSS & SHARE

3 **IN GROUPS** Watch the video and answer the question.

SYM Does advertising work?

In this unit, you will ...

- discuss the advertising of energy drinks, talk about ads that you like and dislike, and debate the effects of advertising.
- use thinking skills: evaluate, symbolize, and induce.
- read about advertising controls around the world.
- use strategies and language to make sure everyone has a turn in a discussion, get a discussion back on track, and paraphrase to clarify what someone has said.
- use media-literacy skills to make a TV ad.
- follow a digital copywriter to learn about this job and the skills needed to be in this industry.

Advertising Regulations

READING

A Are there any ads that you dislike? Why don't you like them?

B 12.01 Read the article. Then answer the questions.

Advertising Around the World: Who Controls What?

As you might expect in the modern world, more and more advertising is being controlled by strict rules. In the US, the Federal Trade Commission (FTC) makes sure that all ads are accurate. In the UK, this is done by the Advertising Standards Agency (ASA), which in 2017 received about 30,000 **complaints** about ads. The job of these agencies is to decide if certain rules are broken by advertisers. **1** ______ The FTC and the ASA decide if the ad can be shown or if it has to be **removed**.

Ads that you might think aren't very offensive can cause lots of complaints. **2** ______ People felt that this ad might encourage bad habits in children. In 2017, another TV ad for fried chicken that showed chickens dancing to rap music was **criticized** for being offensive to vegetarians and vegans. The request was turned down by the ASA.

Each country has different rules about what they allow. A famous series of billboard ads made by a fashionable Italian clothing company caused problems in countries where they appeared. One ad, showing a very young baby, shocked a lot of people. In Sicily, the company was ordered by the town officials to remove the ad. **3** ______ It was given a prize by the Swiss General Poster Association, and a hospital in Bologna asked **permission** to display the ad on its walls.

Some ads have been **banned**, not for showing offensive images, but for the way they market the product. A well-known soft drink ad campaign, which had been seen by millions, was removed for showing a famous celebrity sharing her drink with a police officer at a protest event. **4** ______

GLOSSARY

offensive (adj): causing people to feel upset or embarrassed
billboard (n): a large board for ads in an outside public space

1 What is the name of the organization that controls ads in the US? ______
2 What did viewers not like about the fried chicken ad? ______
3 What type of company produced an ad showing a newborn baby? ______

C READING SKILL—Identify missing sentences Match the sentences (a–d) to lines 1–4 in the article.

a It is interesting that what shocks some people is loved by other people.
b The message is just as important as the image.
c These might include making false promises about the product or using offensive images.
d A TV ad showing people talking with their mouths full of food received the most complaints in the ASA's history.

D THINKING SKILL—Evaluate Consider this statement: "Advertising doesn't really have an effect on the things I choose to buy." Is this statement true for you?

VOCABULARY

A Match the words in bold in READING B with the definitions.

1 ______ (v): officially stated that people must not do or say something
2 ______ (n plural): written or spoken statements in which someone says they are not happy with something
3 ______ (v): said what you thought was bad or wrong about something
4 ______ (n): the right to do something that someone with power gives you
5 ______ (v): taken away from a place

MAKE IT DIGITAL

Research online for examples of ads that have been banned. Do you think that they should have been banned?

GRAMMAR passive voice: other tenses

A Read the examples of the passive voice from READING B. Find five other examples of passive sentences in the article.

... more and more advertising is being controlled by strict rules. (present progressive passive)
The job of these agencies is to decide if certain rules are broken by advertisers. (simple present passive)
... was criticized for being offensive. (simple past passive)
Some ads have been banned ... (present perfect passive)
... which had been seen by millions ... (past perfect passive)

B Choose the correct options.

1. Use the passive voice to show that the action is **more** / **less** important than the person doing the action.
2. Use the passive voice when you **know** / **don't know** who did the action.
3. Only use the passive voice with **transitive** / **intransitive** verbs.

For more practice, go to page 158.

C Complete the text with the correct passive forms of the verbs in parentheses. More than one form may be possible.

An ad for an electronic device **1** ________________ (change) recently following a complaint. Alexa, as she **2** ________________ (know) around the world, tried to order cat food when she heard her name on a cat food ad. The ad, which shows the device **3** ________________ (use) in different situations by different people, confused Alexa into making the order. A complaint **4** ________________ (receive) by an advertising complaints organization. Amazon agreed that Alexa did place an order for the cat food, but the order **5** ________________ (cancel) by the customer. Customers now have to confirm their orders. The orders **6** ________________ (remove) immediately from their shopping carts if customers do not confirm them.

D IN PAIRS Think about a recent ad campaign that you like. Describe it to your partner. Can he or she guess the ad? Who is it made by? Where is it advertised? How long has it been advertised?

This ad is made by a fast food company. It's been shown on TV for about six months, but the actors have been changed recently.

SPEAKING

A IN PAIRS Should energy drinks be advertised on TV and in magazines? Complete the table and give reasons.

For	Against

B IN GROUPS Decide whether you are for or against advertising energy drinks on TV or in magazines. Take turns presenting your opinion and giving reasons. Use the Confident Communicator box to help you.

CONFIDENT COMMUNICATOR
KEEP TALKING

To make sure everyone in a group has a turn in a discussion, use phrases like this:
Can we hear someone else's opinion?
What do you think, [name]?

How Does Advertising Work?

VOCABULARY advertising campaigns

A Match the job responsibilities (1–6) with the meanings (a–f). Use a dictionary if needed.

1 come up with a slogan _____
2 promote a product _____
3 design the logo _____
4 launch the product _____
5 identify the target market _____
6 manage the budget _____

a think of words or phrases to sell a product
b figure out which groups of people will buy a product
c attract people's attention to a product
d start selling a new product
e control the money spent on a project
f create a memorable image connected to a product

LISTENING

A IN PAIRS Look at the magazine ads. What are they trying to tell you about the product? Who is the target market?

B 12.02 Listen to an excerpt from an interview with a marketing executive. What does he consider in ad campaigns? Choose the correct answers.

The man says that …

1 they identify their target market using five / six / seven different categories.
2 in ads for younger people, the music is slower / faster / calmer than in ads for older people.
3 ads for people over the age of 40 / 50 / 60 often have calmer music.
4 the more you write slogans, the harder / the faster / the easier it gets.

C 12.03 LISTENING SKILL—Listen for inference Listen to the ad. Then answer the questions.

1 What is the ad for? ____________________
2 Who is the target market? ____________________
3 Why is the ad appropriate for this market? ____________________
____

D THINKING SKILL—Symbolize Sketch as many logos as you can in two minutes. Why do you think these logos stick in your mind?

GRAMMAR comparative and superlative adverbs

A Look at the phrases in bold in the sentences from LISTENING B. Which adverbs are comparative? Which are superlative? Write C or S.

1 … one of the first things we have to **do the most carefully** is identify our target market. _____
2 And in TV or radio ads directed at older people, the actors usually **speak more seriously** and less quickly. _____
3 "These running shoes will help you **run faster**!" _____

B **Choose the correct options to complete the grammar rules.**

1 Most comparative adverbs are formed with ... + adverb.
  a *more* b *the most*
2 Most superlative adverbs are formed with ... + adverb.
  a *more* b *the most*
3 Most short adverbs, such as *fast* and *hard*, end in *–er* in the comparative and *–est* in the ...
  a superlative. b infinitive.
4 The verb usually goes ... the adverb.
  a before b after

For more practice, go to page 159.

C **Complete the sentences with the correct forms of the words in parentheses.**

1 In commercials for younger people, the actors talk ________________ (quick) than in commercials for older people.
2 Ad campaigns work the ________________ (successful) when they have a clear target market.
3 They're working ________________ (careful) on this ad campaign than the last one.
4 Our products are selling more ________________ (slow) than we'd like them to.
5 The people in that ad sing ________________ (badly) than I thought possible!

MAKE IT REAL

There are different ways of talking about TV *ads*. You can talk about *ads* or *commercials* (all informal) or about *advertisements* (more formal).

D **IN PAIRS Talk about ads.**

Which ones ...
1 do you see most often?
2 work the most successfully?
3 make the product look better than it actually is?

SPEAKING

A **Think about an ad you like and an ad you dislike. Complete the table with notes about them.**

	Ad I Like	Ad I Dislike
Product		
Logo		
Slogan		
Target market		
Kind of ad (print, TV, billboard)		
People, activity, or music in ad		

B **IN GROUPS Talk about ads you like and dislike. Suggest improvements for the ad you dislike. Use the Confident Communicator box to help you.**

A: Why don't you like this commercial?
B: I think the people in the ad speak too quickly. I think they could speak more slowly.

CONFIDENT COMMUNICATOR
REPAIR IT

If a discussion goes "off topic," you can use the phrases to get the discussion back on topic:
Going back to what I was saying earlier about advertising.
Let's get back to talking about how to improve this ad campaign.
You were saying that you didn't like this ad.

LESSON 3 The "Unreal" World of Advertising

VOCABULARY discourse markers

A Write the discourse markers from the box next to the correct functions.

although	as well as	for instance	such as
as a result	due to	in addition	whereas

Function	Examples
Adding information	also, too, and, furthermore, **1** __________, **2** __________
Giving examples	for example, **3** __________, **4** __________
Giving reasons	because, so, therefore, **5** __________, **6** __________
Contrasting different ideas	but, however, on the one hand, on the other hand, **7** __________, **8** __________

B Choose the correct options.

1. A: Do you always change channels when the commercials come on?
   B: Not always, **because** / **although** I actually like watching some of them.
2. A: Did you know that this ad was banned in many countries?
   B: I know. But **in addition** / **as a result**, the fast food chain became even more popular!
3. A: Ads for products **such as** / **due to** soft drinks shouldn't be shown during kids' movies.
   B: I completely agree.
4. A: **As well as** / **Whereas** all the pop-up ads on Facebook, I get a lot of spam email, too.
   B: Yeah, me too. It's really annoying.

LISTENING

A IN PAIRS **Compare the pictures. Which one has been photoshopped (changed to look different)? How do you know?**

B 12.04 LISTENING SKILL—Recognize discourse markers **Listen to four people giving their opinions about advertising. Then match each speaker with the discourse marker that he or she uses (a–d).**

1. Speaker 1: ____
2. Speaker 2: ____
3. Speaker 3: ____
4. Speaker 4: ____

a. due to
b. such as
c. as a result
d. although

GLOSSARY
edit (v): to make changes to a photo to make it look better

C 12.04 Listen again and decide which speaker (1–4) has a positive opinion of advertising and which speaker has a negative opinion.

(+) opinion ____________________

(–) opinion ____________________

D THINKING SKILL—Induce Decide if people generally believe what companies say about their products.

PRONUNCIATION filler sounds and words

A 12.05 Listen to the sentences from LISTENING B. Underline the filler sounds and words that the speakers use. Why do you think they use them?

1. Situations that people can, um, understand and connect with.
2. I felt quite angry, hmm …
3. You might think ad companies would, you know, check the images carefully …
4. It's like, when I'm shopping, what makes me pick up certain things and buy them?

B Think about your language. What filler sounds and words do you use?

WRITING

A Read the essay prompt and one student's answer to it. Has the student answered the question? Why or why not?

PROMPT: "Photoshopped images should be banned in ads." Discuss the arguments for and against this statement.

In recent years, some advertising companies have been criticized for using photoshopped images in their advertising campaigns. For example, it's common for the pictures in ads for some products—beauty products, for instance—to be edited to make the people in the ads appear perfect. The ad companies use computer technology to change the shape of people's bodies. Due to this trend, young people can have health problems because they try to look like the people in the ads. As a result, photoshopping ads has already been banned in some countries. In France, for example, photoshopped images are not shown in magazines or on billboards. I agree that it should now be banned in the rest of the world, too.

B IN PAIRS Can you think of any arguments in favor of photoshopping images in ads? Make notes.

C Write a for-and-against paragraph about photoshopping. Use ideas from A and the notes you made in B. Try to include some discourse markers from VOCABULARY A.

SPEAKING

A What is your opinion on the following question: "Do the images used in advertising have a positive or negative effect on people?" Make notes.

B IN GROUPS Discuss your ideas, giving examples and reasons. Use discourse markers to connect your ideas. Use the Confident Communicator box to help you.

CONFIDENT COMMUNICATOR

KEEP TALKING

Use the following phrases to paraphrase and clarify what someone else has said in a debate or discussion:

So, what you're saying is that these ads make people feel uncomfortable?

Am I right in thinking that you think ads do have a negative effect on people?

If I understand correctly, you're saying that ads don't have any negative effects?

Language and Life

Media Literacy – A TV ad

A 12.06 **When a company has an idea for a TV ad, they make a storyboard. Read the article and then choose the correct options.**

STORYBOARDS: WHAT YOU NEED TO KNOW

A Simple Guide

Have you ever come up with the most fantastic idea for an ad—or perhaps a home-made video—but had a problem getting your ideas down on paper? Then you need a storyboard!

WHAT IS A STORYBOARD?

A storyboard is a series of sketches, drawn in the style of a comic. It shows every scene of the ad. It shows what characters are in the scene, what they are doing, and what they are saying. A good storyboard will help you imagine the ad. It shows the production team what to photograph and in what order. It communicates ideas without long, wordy descriptions. As more people become involved in making the ad and give their opinions, the storyboard may develop and change.

HOW TO MAKE A STORYBOARD

A storyboard doesn't have to be complicated. Here's how to make one:

STEP 1: MAKE A TEMPLATE

Draw a series of **squares** or **rectangles** on a plain piece of paper, one for each scene. Leave room underneath the squares or rectangles for notes. You can also find free storyboards online.

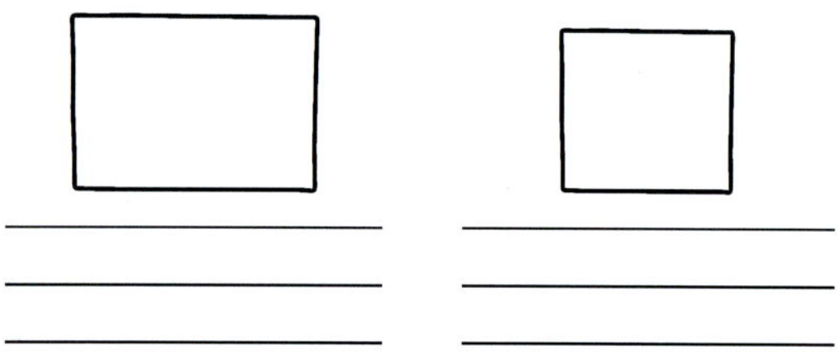

STEP 2: DRAW THE STORY

Don't worry if you aren't very good at drawing. You can use **simple stick figures** in the boxes. Show any movement with an **arrow** or **short parallel lines**.

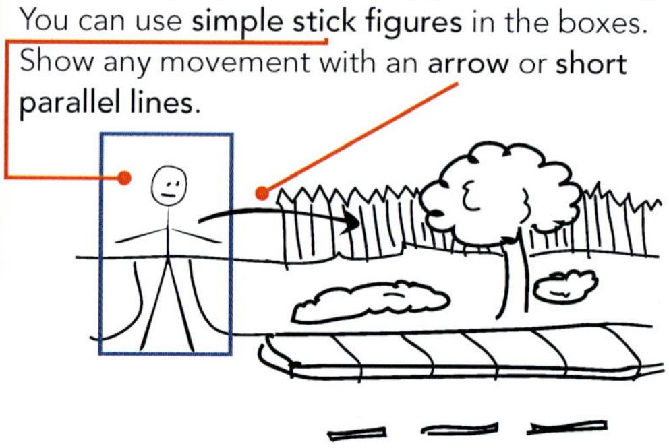

"Hey! Wait for me!"

Camera: Pans to the right from this angle as person walks. *Background music: Should have an upbeat tempo.*

STEP 3: ADD THE DIALOGUE

Write any dialogue underneath the pictures. You can also make a silent video where no dialogue is necessary.

STEP 4: ADD NOTES

These might include instructions for camera angles, descriptions of the actions in the scene, or ideas for music.

Good luck!

1 You make a storyboard at the start / end of an ad campaign.
2 A storyboard contains long / short written descriptions.
3 You need / don't need to be a good artist to draw a storyboard.
4 Storyboards have to / don't have to include dialogue.

B **IN PAIRS** **Look at the storyboard for an ad. Take turns describing what you think is happening in each of the scenes.**

C **IN PAIRS** **Discuss the following questions.**

1 What product do you think the ad is trying to sell?
2 Who is the biggest market?
3 What message is the ad trying to communicate?
4 Do you think the ad works? Why or why not?

D **IN GROUPS** **Make a storyboard for a TV ad.**

1 Choose a product. It can be real or imaginary.
2 Identify the target market.
3 Discuss your ideas and message for a TV ad.
4 Make a storyboard for a TV ad.

MAKE IT DIGITAL

Turn your storyboard idea into an ad. Decide which parts you are playing, practice any dialogue, and record your ad!

E **Present your storyboards as a class.**

F **Discuss the questions.**

1 Whose ad do you think would be the most successful. Why?
2 What are the key factors of a successful ad?

VOCABULARY review

SCORE: / 10

A Complete the text with words or phrases from the box.

although | as a result | budget | comes up with | identify | in addition | launch | logo | such as | whereas

My job is to manage ad campaigns for a large grocery store. We need to develop an ad campaign for party food **1** ________________ snacks and drinks. **2** ________________ in the past, ads for food were designed to appeal mostly to women, nowadays we have to **3** ________________ our target market more carefully. **4** ________________, we spend a lot more time researching who buys our products. The creative team **5** ________________ a slogan for the new ad and the design team makes the **6** ________________ that goes on our party food packaging. **7** ________________, I have to manage the **8** ________________ to make sure we don't spend too much money. Today, we will have a meeting to discuss how we are going to **9** ________________ a new product in the market. **10** ________________ the different teams sometimes disagree about the best way to advertise a product, we usually produce a great ad!

GRAMMAR review

SCORE: / 10

A Rewrite the sentences using the passive voice in your notebook.

1. They showed this ad for the first time this year.
2. An artist designed that logo.
3. Some governments have banned that ad.
4. We are launching the product in the early fall.
5. The creative team had developed the storyboard.

B Choose the correct options.

1. Ed is **the harder** / **the hardest** worker on the design team.
2. The man in the soap ad sings **more beautifully** / **the beautifullest** than the woman.
3. Aiden draws **more slow** / **more slowly** than Mark.
4. Melanie presented her ideas **more confidently** / **most confidently** than Juan.
5. The ad campaign for cookies worked **most** / **more** successfully than that for brownies.

16–20 correct: You can talk about advertising and advertising campaigns. You can use the passive voice and comparative and superlative adverbs.
0–15 correct: Look again at the Vocabulary and Grammar sections in the unit.

TOTAL SCORE: / 20

WHAT DO YOU KNOW NOW? Look back at page 117 and add the words you know now to the box.

FOLLOW A PRO ADVERTISING

Take the quiz about advertising. Go to Follow A Pro on page 134 to find the answers. Then learn about advertising.

1 What did the first ad shown on British TV advertise?
a dog food **b** toothpaste **c** hamburgers

2 Pepsi's TV ad campaign in 2002 was the most expensive ever. How much did it cost?
a $8.1 million **b** $81 million **c** $108 million

3 What event did the first billboard ad in New York advertise?
a a circus **b** a baseball game **c** a music performance

4 In most wristwatch ads, what time is shown on the watch?
a 8:40 **b** 10:10 **c** 12:00

UNIT 7

STUDY SKILLS

A Read the essay. Which of the questions is the writer trying to answer? What is your answer to that question?

STRUCTURING YOUR WRITING

a Describe a time you made a serious mistake. What did you learn from it?
b If you don't make mistakes, you'll never learn. In your opinion, is this true?

Consider the achievements of the last hundred years. People have gone to space, invented the internet, and made incredible breakthroughs in medicine. Is it possible that in each of these attempts, the first try was successful? Of course not. We know that these achievements were only possible through trial and error—in other words, through making countless mistakes.

It's important to remember this in our own lives. Often, we believe that we need to do everything right the first time. This belief is generated by the images of perfection in magazines, on TV, and on social media.

However, this desire to get everything right the first time is dangerous. Take a man who has just started to play the violin, for example. How many wrong notes will he have to play before he plays something that is enjoyable to listen to? Or a woman who is learning to juggle? How many balls will she drop before she keeps them all in the air?

People who aspire to live a life free from mistakes will never take risks, never challenge themselves, and never learn anything new. They will turn down opportunities to avoid looking a fool. This will result in a safe life free from embarrassment and risk, but it will also result in regret at wasted opportunities.

Mistakes are seen as a form of failure but they can be really positive. Mistakes help us learn, and it is for this reason that I believe that they are not just important but desirable.

B Read the essay again. Check (✓) the correct sentences.

1 ☐ The essay is organized into paragraphs.
2 ☐ Each paragraph contains several different ideas.
3 ☐ The writer develops a clear argument, moving logically from point to point.
4 ☐ The writer doesn't provide any evidence to support her ideas.
5 ☐ The writer begins with an introduction and ends with a conclusion.

C Match the headings (1–4) to the tips for structuring essays (a–d). Then write your own tips under each heading in your notebook.

1 Divide your main idea into topics ____
2 Rearrange your notes ____
3 Write an outline plan ____
4 Organize the information into paragraphs ____

a Use separate sheets of paper for each topic.
b Plan your introduction, conclusion, and the main body of your essay.
c Each paragraph should have one main idea with supporting details or evidence.
d Spread your notes out on the table so that you can easily see them.

D IN PAIRS Think about the last essay you wrote. Tell your partner about the process you went through to structure your essay. What would you do differently next time?

E THINKING SKILLS—Apply What do you find most challenging about structuring an essay? How can you develop this skill for future assignments?

✓ MAKE IT HAPPEN

Choose one of the essay questions in **A** and write a short essay (500 words maximum) with your main idea divided into topics, each in their own paragraph.

Answers to the quiz on page 76
1 b 2 3, 4, 1, 5, 2 3 a, b, c

UNIT 8 FOLLOW A PRO

A Read about an astrobiologist. Then choose *True* or *False*.

AN ASTROBIOLOGIST

I'm an astrobiologist, which might sound like a job in a science-fiction movie! Actually, it's not science fiction. Astrobiologists study if life exists in other places in the universe besides Earth. We study how life originated, and how life could exist in extreme environments. There is an enormous variety in the jobs astrobiologists do. Some develop computer models to predict what life would be like on other planets. Others study life in extreme climates like the freezing Arctic, the Atacama Desert, or the deepest oceans. Some astrobiologists use high-tech radio telescopes to listen for signals from aliens. To be honest, I think that would be boring because so far, all the communication from outer space has come from our own satellites. Most astrobiologists work in an office or a lab and do research on elements like carbon, nitrogen, phosphorus, and iron. The results of the research help create the computer models that predict whether a specific planet or solar system could have life.

To work in astrobiology, you need a degree in a related field such as biology, chemistry, physics, astronomy, geology, mathematics, or information technology. You might think that all astrobiologists work at NASA in the US, but in fact, there are astrobiology jobs in many other parts of the world, including Europe, Australia, Mexico, and South America. There are jobs with NASA projects, at universities, or at private foundations. If you are interested in the origin of life, and the possibility of life on other planets, astrobiology might be the career for you.

1 Astrobiologists mostly work in science-fiction movies. True / False
2 Astrobiologists study the history of life. True / False
3 There are many different types of jobs in astrobiology. True / False
4 The writer thinks listening for alien communications is an exciting job. True / False
5 You have to live in the US to work in astrobiology. True / False

B Discuss the questions as a class.

1 Why do you think the writer says that astrobiology sounds like a job in a science-fiction movie?
2 Would any of the astrobiology jobs mentioned in the article interest you? If so, which ones?

VIDEO

WATCH THE VIDEO AND FOLLOW AN ASTRONOMER.

C IN GROUPS Answer the questions.

1 What is the person's job? __________
2 Where does the person work? __________
3 What skills does the person need for the job? __________
4 What specific subjects does the person study for the job? __________
5 Why does the person use special equipment in the job? __________
6 What does the person say is the best part of the job? __________

D IN GROUPS Check your answers to the quiz on page 86 and discuss the questions.

1 If you had a lot of money, would you want to be a "space tourist"? Why or why not?
2 What do you think the most important reasons for space exploration are?

Answers to the quiz on page 86
1 b 2 a 3 c 4 c

STUDY SKILLS

A **Esme and Marley are taking a course on the history of popular music. Read their notes about Motown music. Whose notes are more likely to be an effective study aid?**

MAKING NOTES

1 Esme

Motown is often described as "the sound that changed America." It was founded by an American songwriter called Berry Gordy (?) who got a loan of $800 (?) from his family to set the company up with. He wanted to set the record company up in recognition of the warm, soulful, and talented people he grew up with. Motown success stories included Smokey Robinson & The Miracles, Michael Jackson and the Jackson 5, Marvin Gaye, Diana Ross & The Supremes (?), and many more.

Motown was the first African American record label to achieve widespread recognition and acclaim.

2 Marley

From Billy Robson's "Sound of America," pps 35–37

Motown founded by Am. songwriter Berry Gordy from Detroit—1st Af/Am label to achieve widespread acclaim

Detroit called Motor City=name Motown

Acts: Smokey Robinson & Miracles, Michael Jackson & Jkson 5, Diana Ross & Supremes, etc.

B **Write *E* (Esme) or *M* (Marley).**

1 The writer has noted down the sources. ____
2 The writer has tried to copy down every word. ____
3 The writer has highlighted the most important information. ____
4 The writer is not totally sure how correct the notes are. ____

C **Match the sentence halves to make tips about taking notes.**

1 Before you start making notes, ____
2 Make a list of questions you want to find answers to ____
3 It's a good idea to label and number pages ____
4 Use sticky notes so that you can ____
5 Use abbreviations because this will ____

a draw up a mind map so you can see what you already know about the subject.
b write down ideas as you think of them or add ideas to charts or posters.
c save you a lot of time.
d as this will make it easier to cross-reference your notes.
e as this will make your notes more focused.

D IN PAIRS **Think about notes you have taken from lectures or books. How could you improve your note-taking technique?**

E THINKING SKILLS—Apply **What do you find hardest about taking notes? How can you ensure that your notes are as effective as possible?**

MAKE IT HAPPEN

Go online and find a podcast on a subject that interests you. Take notes using the tips from **C**. When the podcast has finished, look at your notes. How can you make them clearer? How can you make the key information stand out?

Answers to the quiz on page 96
1 b 2 b 3 b; Use symbols and abbreviations in notes, but not in assignments. 4 a; Visual familiarity will help you to remember the content of your notes.

UNIT 10 FOLLOW A PRO

A Read about a talent scout's job. Answer the questions below.

A TALENT SCOUT

Meet Jeni Mills, a talent scout from Chicago.
Jeni says: "I started out working in theater production for musical shows on Broadway, which was a fantastic job to go to after college, where I majored in music and dance. But then I decided I wanted a change. I saw an ad for an international cruise ship company that was looking for a talent scout to find the best acts for their cruise ship shows. These shows are really popular, and the audience expects to see something special. While I know a lot of people in the entertainment industry from my work on Broadway, I want to find acts that are a little different, but still amazing. So, a few times a week I go to small gigs—shows at small theaters and local comedy and music clubs—and try to find the most talented people. I organize auditions and get the best acts to come back and try to impress a live theater audience before we offer them work on the ship. I've found wonderful magicians and amazing dancers, singers, and comedians. I've been doing the job for five years now and I love it. The only negative is that the hours are long, but I'm meeting interesting people all the time."

1 What job did Jeni do before she became a talent scout? ______
2 What did Jeni study in college? ______
3 Where does Jeni find the acts for her shows? ______
4 How long has Jeni been working as a talent scout? ______
5 What does Jeni not like about her job? ______

B Discuss the questions as a class.

1 Would you like to be a talent scout? Why or why not?
2 What do you think it would be like to work on a cruise ship?

VIDEO

WATCH THE VIDEO AND FOLLOW A MUSICIAN.

C IN GROUPS Answer the questions.

1 What does the person do? ______
2 What skills does the person need for the job? ______
3 What is the person's schedule? ______
4 How many instruments does the person play? ______
5 What is the person's favorite music style? ______
6 What is the most exciting part of the person's job? ______

D IN GROUPS Check your answers to the quiz on page 106 and discuss the questions.

1 Do you know anybody who works in the entertainment industry? If so, what do they do?
2 What kinds of live entertainment are popular in your country?
3 What skills do you think a talent scout needs?
4 What type of acts (e.g., music, dance, comedy, magic) do you think require the most talent? Why?
5 Can you think of any professions other than the entertainment industry where talent scouts work? If so, what are they?

Answers to the quiz on page 106
1 b 2 a 3 c 4 c

STUDY SKILLS

A Read the conversation. Is this study session productive? What challenges are the friends facing?

PERSONAL DEVELOPMENT

Marco: Ah, I love study nights! It's so much more fun than reviewing my notes on my own. More pizza, anyone?
Jill: Yeah, it is good fun, Marco, but we need to focus now.
Liz: Sure, Jill. We can't let this delicious pizza get cold, though, can we?
Jill: I guess not … It's just that the exam is in only two weeks.
Marco: We're probably going to fail it, Jill. No one does well in Mr. Leaper's class.
Liz: Yeah. He's right. I guess we can try again next year, though, right?
Jill: Don't say that! I've been trying to study all month. This is my first night out of the house in weeks!
Liz: Hmm. You are looking really pale, Jill. Are you eating well?
Jill: I don't have time to eat! And I'm not hungry, to be honest. I'm way too stressed out.
Marco: Well, I studied all day yesterday. I sat at my desk for six hours. I'm not sure if I learned much, though. The view from my window is pretty cool …
Liz: Lucky you, having the time to look out the window! I'm just so busy … Getting the bus to work, working, looking after my brother. He's been sick this week, so I've been taking care of him …
Marco: Yeah, if only we had more time! Speaking of time, that new series everyone is talking about starts in 10 minutes. I know we haven't finished but we've done a lot, right?

B Which student would benefit from each piece of advice? Write *M* (Marco), *J* (Jill), or *L* (Liz).

1 Add your favorite TV shows to your timetable. Use TV shows as a reward for finishing a study session. ____
2 Surround yourself with people who are positive and will encourage you. ____
3 Seek help from a professional counselor at college if you feel you can't deal with things. ____
4 Always carry your notes with you and study on the bus or while you wait. ____
5 Study with friends if you struggle to study alone, but make sure you use the time constructively. For example, explain something to your friend and see how well your friend understands your explanation. ____
6 Keep an exam question in your head and write points down as they occur to you. ____

C Match each piece of advice (1–4) to a way to follow it (a–d).

1 Get organized and focused. ____
2 Manage your time carefully. ____
3 Stay healthy. ____
4 Use exam papers from past years. ____

a Brainstorm answers to past questions.
b Create a realistic schedule.
c Include regular exercise in your schedule.
d Make flashcards with key information.

D IN PAIRS Role-play the study session in A. Make it more positive and productive.

Lucille: Why don't we take a break and have some ice cream?
Rob: Why don't we wait until we've finished this chapter? Hey, can I try explaining what I've just read to see if I've understood it?
Lucille: Sure!

E THINKING SKILLS—Apply What do you find hardest about studying for tests? What are your challenges, and how can you improve your study habits?

MAKE IT HAPPEN

Talk about your study habits with your partner. Share what you think you are doing well and talk about the areas you need to improve.

Answers to the quiz on page 116
1 a 2 b; It can be very effective. 3 c 4 a

UNIT 12

FOLLOW A PRO

A **Read about a digital copywriter's job. Answer the questions below in your notebook.**

A DIGITAL COPYWRITER

There are many different jobs in advertising. Bruno Torres is a digital copywriter. He tells us more about his career.

Bruno says: "People are always asking me what a digital copywriter's job is. I think it's because it's one of those "behind the scenes" jobs. It's a very important job—especially for the advertising industry. My team develops advertising campaigns. My main job is to check all of the online materials—the headlines, slogans, emails, and social media ads. I check spelling and grammar, obviously, but I also make sure that the advertising material is easy to understand and that it sells the product! I usually work on at least two or three projects for different campaigns at the same time, so I need to be focused and organized. It's also very important that I meet my deadlines and finish the work by a certain date. Advertising is about creating trends so I have to make sure I know what is important to young people—style, fashion, how things look—that's a major part of it. People don't just buy a product—they buy into a lifestyle. People also ask how I got started in my career. Well, I majored in media studies and worked as a journalist for three years. Then I changed to this career because it seems more interesting. I hope to become a creative director one day and be in charge of the whole advertising campaign from start to finish."

1. Why do people often ask Bruno what a digital copywriter's job is?
2. What is the main part of Bruno's job?
3. How many projects does Bruno usually work on?
4. What job did Bruno do before he became a digital copywriter?
5. What does Bruno want to do in the future?

B **Discuss the questions as a class.**

1. Would you like to work in advertising? Why or why not?
2. What would you like about being a digital copywriter? What would you dislike? Explain.

VIDEO

WATCH THE VIDEO AND FOLLOW A VIDEO EDITOR.

C **IN GROUPS Answer the questions.**

1. What is the person's job? ______
2. Where does the person work? ______
3. What skills does the person need for the job? ______
4. What are the person's main responsibilities? ______
5. Has the person worked with someone famous? If yes, who? ______
6. What does the person say is the best part of the job? ______

D **IN GROUPS Check your answers to the quiz on page 126 and discuss the questions.**

1. How important do you think good language skills are to a digital copywriter's job?
2. What other skills do you think a digital copywriter needs?
3. Would you be good at a job with deadlines? Why or why not?
4. What advertising campaigns have succeeded in your country? Why?
5. What is the most effective medium for advertising: TV, magazines, the internet, billboards, or something else?

Answers to the quiz on page 126
1 b 2 a 3 a 4 b

Irregular Verbs

Infinitive	Simple past	Past participle
be	was/were	been
become	became	become
begin	began	begun
break	broke	broken
bring	brought	brought
build	built	built
buy	bought	bought
catch	caught	caught
choose	chose	chosen
come	came	come
cost	cost	cost
cut	cut	cut
do	did	done
draw	drew	drawn
drink	drank	drunk
drive	drove	driven
eat	ate	eaten
fall	fell	fallen
feed	fed	fed
feel	felt	felt
find	found	found
fly	flew	flown
get	got	gotten
give	gave	given
go	went	gone
grow	grew	grown
hang	hung	hung
have	had	had
hear	heard	heard
hit	hit	hit
hold	held	held
hurt	hurt	hurt
keep	kept	kept
know	knew	known
leave	left	left
let	let	let
lose	lost	lost
make	made	made
meet	met	met
pay	paid	paid
put	put	put
read	read	read
ride	rode	ridden
ring	rang	rung
rise	rose	risen
run	ran	run
say	said	said
see	saw	seen
sell	sold	sold
send	sent	sent
set	set	set
sing	sang	sung
sit	sat	sat
speak	spoke	spoken
stand	stood	stood
stick	stuck	stuck
take	took	taken
teach	taught	taught
tell	told	told
think	thought	thought
throw	threw	thrown
understand	understood	understood
wake	woke	woken
wear	wore	worn
win	won	won
write	wrote	written

Pronunciation Symbols

Vowels

ɪ	did
ɛ	bed
æ	bad
ʌ	cup
ʊ	book
ə	banana
i	feed
ɑ	father, box
ɔ	tall
u	student, food
ɚ	shirt, birthday
eɪ	date, table
aɪ	cry, eye
ɔɪ	boy
oʊ	comb, post
aʊ	about, how

Consonants

p	park, happy
b	back, hobby
t	tea
d	die
k	came, kitchen, quarter
g	game, go
f	face, photographer
v	vegetable
θ	thing, math
ð	then, that
s	city, summer
z	please, goes
ʃ	she, shop
ʒ	leisure
h	hot, who
tʃ	chicken, watch
dʒ	jacket, orange
m	men
n	sun, know
ŋ	sung, singer
w	week, white
r	rain, writer
l	light, long
j	yes, use, music

Grammar Review

A Complete the news report with the simple past or the past progressive form of the verbs in parentheses.

There was a fire last night at 10:20 p.m. on East Coast Road. While Jon and Lisa Hawes **1** ______________ (watch) TV in their living room, their five-year-old son **2** ______________ (play) with matches in his bedroom. He **3** ______________ (light) a small fire and then, afraid, **4** ______________ (run) into the bathroom. While his parents **5** ______________ (come) to check on him, they **6** ______________ (smell) smoke. They **7** ______________ (try) to put the fire out, but it was already too big. They found their son, **8** ______________ (call) the fire department, and got out of the house safely.

B Choose the correct options.

Tyler: I really like your apartment. It gets **1** any / a lot of light.

Miguel: Yeah, but there isn't **2** enough / too many space for all my stuff. And I'd like to move **3** somebody / somewhere closer to school.

Tyler: But this is a great neighborhood. There are **4** some / any great restaurants and cafés here.

Miguel: I know, but there's **5** too many / too much noise around here on the weekends. It feels like **6** anybody / everyone is out on the street at night.

Tyler: You live alone, right? Have you ever thought about getting a roommate?

Miguel: I've considered it **7** a few / a little times, but I really like living by **8** myself / ourselves.

C Complete the sentences with the correct superlative form of the adjective in parentheses.

1 My cat is the ______________ (lazy) animal I've ever seen.
2 That was the ______________ (risk) thing I've ever done.
3 Rush hour is the ______________ (bad) time to get a seat on the bus.
4 Craig is the ______________ (creative) person in class.
5 Maria is the ______________ (kind) of my three sisters.
6 Ines is the ______________ (good) person to have as a study partner.

D Rewrite the sentences to include the verb in parentheses.

1 You are not allowed to come in. (can't)

____

2 Do you want to go with me? (would)

____

3 I'll possibly be late to the ceremony. (may)

____

4 Will you book a hotel room for me? (could)

____

5 I don't think I'll be able to come. (might)

____

6 Our flight lands in 30 minutes. (will)

____

E **Complete the sentences with the simple past or the present perfect form of the verb in parentheses.**

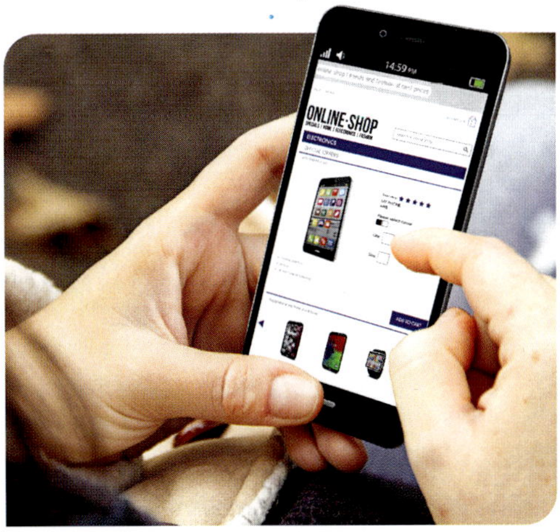

Although he is just a teenager, Brandon Iverson **1** ___________ (be) a businessman for much of his life. At age 10, he and a friend **2** ___________ (sell) old toys and games online. When he was 13, they **3** ___________ (establish) their own financial education company. A year later, they **4** ___________ (publish) a book on how to succeed as a young entrepreneur. They **5** ___________ (make) a lot of money since then. A few years ago, Brandon **6** ___________ (start) another online company selling T-shirts, jogging pants, and hoodies. The company **7** ___________ (do) well since its launch. Recently, he **8** ___________ (become) a popular speaker at schools around the country, and he is enjoying this new venture.

F **Unscramble and write the sentences.**

1 Jesse / degree / gotten / yet / hasn't / his / .

____

2 ever / Lila / promotion / a / gotten / has / ?

____

3 here / since / worked / 2017 / has / Peter / .

____

4 applied / Erica / for / already / job / has / the / .

____

5 our / read / I / just / benefits / about / have / .

____

6 been / Tina / has / month / team / a / leader / for / .

____

G **Choose the correct option.**

1 Many people are interested in **cooking** / **to cook** these days.
2 Why doesn't Claire want **flying** / **to fly** a kite with her friends?
3 Henri enjoys **making** / **to make** things with wood.
4 David really dislikes **cleaning** / **to clean** his apartment.
5 We really hope **seeing** / **to see** you at the park this weekend.
6 **Having** / **To have** a potluck meal sounds like a great idea!
7 Where did you and Ethan decide **going** / **to go** last night?
8 Would you like **coming** / **to come** over for a barbecue tonight?

H **Complete the sentences with the correct form of the verb in parentheses.**

1 Fur coats ___________ (not wear) much nowadays.
2 Children may develop health problems if they ___________ (eat) too much food.
3 These days, most hotel reservations ___________ (make) online.
4 If we ___________ (not be) friends, I would be angry with you.
5 When my parents were young, milk ___________ (sell) in bottles.
6 If the weather doesn't improve, we ___________ (not have) a picnic.
7 Cotton ___________ (use) in clothing such as blue jeans and T-shirts.
8 I ___________ (meet) my cousin at the airport tomorrow.

UNIT 7 — *should/shouldn't have*

Function

We use *should* + (*not*) + *have* + past participle to talk about past regrets. We often use it to give advice or a recommendation about something that did or did not happen in the past.

Form

Form and Use	Example
Use *should have* + past participle when something didn't happen in the past, but it was a good idea.	He should have listened carefully. (= He didn't listen carefully.) They should have apologized. (= They didn't apologize.)
Use *shouldn't have* + past participle when something happened in the past, but it was a bad idea.	She shouldn't have told a lie. (= She told a lie.) They shouldn't have said those things. (= They said those things.)

A Match the statements (1–6) to the responses (a–f).

1 She spilled coffee on her computer. ____
2 They told me about my surprise party. ____
3 She bought a leather jacket for $600. ____
4 They were very late for the meeting. ____
5 She kept her library books too long. ____
6 They bought 30 lottery tickets. ____

a They should have been there on time.
b She should have been more careful.
c She should have returned them sooner.
d She shouldn't have spent so much.
e They shouldn't have wasted their money.
f They shouldn't have let me know.

B Complete the sentences with *should have* or *shouldn't have* and the past participle of the verb in parentheses.

In 1997, a Canadian beverage company introduced a soda called Orbitz. The product's appearance looked attractive, but the taste wasn't very popular. It was removed from sale a year later.

1 The company ____________________ (make) it taste better.
2 The company ____________________ (spend) so much money on the product's appearance.
3 The company ____________________ (try) to promote it in different ways.

In 2000, Netflix suggested that they manage Blockbuster's online component, while Blockbuster continued to sell videos in its stores. Blockbuster said no and went bankrupt, while Netflix continues to thrive.

4 Blockbuster ____________________ (take) Netflix's offer more seriously.
5 Blockbuster ____________________ (refuse) Netflix's offer.
6 Blockbuster ____________________ (accept) Netflix's offer.

KFC's advertising slogan in the US has been "Finger Lickin' Good" since the 1950s. When it was translated into Putonghua for the Chinese market, it was translated as "Eat Your Fingers Off."

7 KFC ____________________ (get) a better translator.
8 KFC ____________________ (use) a different slogan for the Chinese market.
9 KFC ____________________ (test) the translation on a few people in the Chinese market.

UNIT 7 — past perfect for wishes about the past

Function

We use *wish* + past perfect to talk about wishes or regrets about the past. We use this when we want to be able to change a situation in the past, but cannot do so.

Form

Affirmative	Negative
I wish I had saved more money for college. He wishes he had gotten better grades in school. They wish they had bought a better car.	I wish I hadn't said that. Juan wishes he hadn't eaten so much. They wish their neighbors hadn't gotten a dog.

A Complete the sentences with *had* or *hadn't* and the past participle form of the verb in parentheses.

1 Susan's hair is too short. She wishes she ______________ (cut) it.
2 My cousins pay too much in rent. They wish they ______________ (move) somewhere cheaper.
3 Bob's gym membership is expensive. He wishes he ______________ (get) his own gym equipment to use at home.
4 I don't like my meal. I wish I ______________ (order) something else.
5 My sister returned my skirt with holes in it. I wish I ______________ (lend) it to her.
6 Ellen's not comfortable at the party. She wishes she ______________ (come).
7 The Smiths bought their son a desktop computer. He wishes they ______________ (buy) a laptop.
8 This sweater is really hot. I wish I ______________ (wear) a T-shirt.

B Find and correct one error in each sentence.

1 I wish I had live off campus in college. ______________
2 He wish he hadn't gotten married so late. ______________
3 She wishes her parents had allow her to go to the party. ______________
4 They wish they gotten to know their old neighbors better. ______________
5 I wish I hadn't sit at the back of the class. ______________

UNIT 8 — third conditional

Function

We use the third conditional to talk about events that did not happen in the past. They are hypothetical, so we imagine the effects of past conditions that did not happen. The verb in the *if* clause is in the past perfect, and the verb in the main clause is *would/could/might have* + past participle.

Form

Form	Example
If + (subject) + *had* + past participle, (subject) + *would/could/might* + *have* + past participle.	If he had gone to the space station, it would have been a dream come true.
If + (subject) + *had* + past participle, (subject) + *would/could/might* + *not have* + past participle.	If Anna had realized there were so few jobs in astrophysics, she wouldn't have chosen that career.
If + (subject) + *hadn't* + past participle, (subject) + *would/could/might* + *have* + past participle.	If he hadn't been bad at science, he could have become an astronaut.
If + (subject) + *hadn't* + past participle, (subject) + *would/could/might* + *not have* + past participle.	If she hadn't passed the fitness test, she wouldn't have gone into space.

A Choose the correct option.

1 We **won't** / **wouldn't** have learned as much about dinosaurs if we hadn't found so many fossils.
2 If our course had made learning about dinosaurs fun, I would **learn** / **have learned** more.
3 If they **would have** / **had** located the dinosaur skull, it would have been on the news.
4 They might **find** / **have found** more fossils if they had stayed on-site longer.
5 If the dinosaur **had** / **might have** been any bigger, it wouldn't have fit in the museum.
6 The movie might not have been so popular if they **didn't use** / **hadn't used** so many special effects.

B Complete the third conditional sentences with the correct form of the verb in parentheses. Use *would* in the main clause.

1 The space station ______ (not be) a success if we ______ (not work) together.
2 If they ______ (not abandon) the rocket launch, it ______ (be) a disaster.
3 The dinosaurs ______ (not die out) if a meteorite ______ (not hit) the Earth.
4 He ______ (not make) that mistake if he ______ (follow) the instructions.
5 If NASA ______ (not invest) in the space program, astronauts ______ (not go) to the moon.
6 If the Mars rovers ______ (crash), we ______ (not get) such amazing pictures.

UNIT 8 — indirect questions

Function

Direct questions usually begin with an auxiliary verb (*does*, *is*), a modal verb (*can*, *should*), or a *wh-* word (*what*, *where*). Indirect questions are more formal and polite. We use them when we speak to someone we don't know well, or in more formal or professional settings. They begin with phrases that help "soften" the question.

Form

Use	Direct question	Indirect question
In an indirect *wh-* question with *be*, *be* goes after the subject.	How old is the space station?	Do you know how old the space station is?
In other indirect *wh-* questions, there are no auxiliary verbs (e.g., *do*, *does*, *did*).	Where does an astronaut sleep?	Can you tell me where an astronaut sleeps?
In indirect *yes/no* questions, *if* or *whether* is added.	Does it get hot in space?	Do you know whether it gets hot in space?
In indirect *yes/no* questions with a modal, *if* or *whether* is added.	Can people live on Mars?	Could you explain if people can live on Mars?

A Use direct questions to complete the indirect questions about travel to Mars.

1 Who will go from Earth to Mars? Do you know ______?
2 Is it a one-way trip? Can you tell us ______?
3 How long does it take to get to Mars? Do you have any idea ______?
4 Can people on Mars grow their own food? Do you know ______?
5 How did you become interested in Mars? Can you tell us ______?
6 Have you ever seen a spacecraft? Could you please tell us ______?

UNIT 9 — *so, such, too, enough*

Function

Words like *so*, *such*, *too*, and *enough* are used to add emphasis and to indicate degree.

Form

Form and Use	Example
Use *so* + adjective/adverb to mean "very."	It was so kind of you to publish my story.
Use *such* + (article) + adjective + noun to mean "very."	That is such great work! That was such an interesting story.
Use *too* + adjective/adverb to say there is more than is needed.	The print in this newspaper is too small.
Use adjective/adverb + *enough* to say there is the right amount.	The vocabulary in this news article is easy enough.
Use *not* + adjective/adverb + *enough* to say there is less than is needed.	Those sources are not reliable enough.

A Choose the correct option.

It may be **1 too / enough** early to say that traditional news is dead, but things are changing **2 so / such** fast. Journalism is **3 so / such** an amazing field to work in, and I am **4 so / too** proud to work in print media. But our paper is not big **5 such / enough** to survive the competition from citizen journalists. It's becoming **6 too / enough** hard. We traditional journalists simply cannot get our stories out fast **7 too / enough**. I hope most of us will survive **8 such / enough** hard times.

B Complete the sentences with words from the box.

enough so such too

1 Fake news is ______________ a big problem these days.
2 Sometimes it is ______________ hard to tell real news from fake news.
3 Many people believe what they read much ______________ easily.
4 Some people are not critical ______________ of what they read or hear.

UNIT 9 — modals of deduction

Function

Making a deduction means using the information available to guess or draw a conclusion about something. Modals of deduction include *must*, *could*, *might*, *may*, and *can't*. We use these modals to express how sure we are about something in the present.

Form

Form and Use	Example
Use *must* + verb when you are very sure that something is true because there is strong evidence for it.	That story must be true. The author is well known and always trustworthy.
Use *may / might / could* + verb when you think something is possibly true, but there is not enough evidence to be certain.	That story may/might/could be fake. There isn't a source and the writing seems very biased.
Use *can't* + verb when you are very sure that something is not true because there is strong evidence against it.	That story can't be true. Every story on this website has already been proven to be fake.

A Match the sentence halves to make deductions.

1 Pedro slept only an hour last night. He ____
2 Diana owns six cars. She ____
3 Bianca got 100% on her exam. She ____
4 Bryan isn't at his desk. He ____
5 Caroline is wiping her eyes. She ____
6 Kendra is out of the country now. That ____
7 Eric just ate a big lunch. He ____
8 Victor just moved to this city. He ____

a can't be hungry again.
b might be at home.
c could be upset about something.
d can't know many people yet.
e must have a lot of money.
f must be tired.
g can't be her.
h must be happy.

B Choose the correct option.

1 Tim is a professional soccer player. He **must** / **may** be in great shape.
2 There's something bright in the sky. It **must** / **could** be a spaceship.
3 My phone battery **must** / **can't** be dead. I just charged it 10 minutes ago.
4 You **must** / **can't** know David. You were in the same class together.
5 My car won't start. It **must** / **may** not have enough gas.
6 I can't find Eduardo anywhere. He **might** / **can't** be at home.

UNIT 10 — reported speech: statements

Function

When we report what someone says using a verb in the past, the tense of the reported sentence often shifts to one of the past tenses.

Form

Tense shift in reported statements	Direct statement	Reported statement
simple present ➔ simple past	Josh has a lot of talent.	She said (that) Josh had a lot of talent.
present progressive ➔ past progressive	Allie is playing the drums.	He told me (that) Allie was playing the drums.
simple past ➔ past perfect	Mark auditioned for the part.	They stated (that) Mark had auditioned for the part.
present perfect ➔ past perfect	Cecile has not been on TV before.	She admitted (that) Cecile had not been on TV before.
future with *will* ➔ *would*	Ina will win the competition.	They predicted (that) Ina would win the competition.

A Read the situation and complete the sentences using reported speech.

You missed the planning meeting for the school talent show. Your friend Sheila attended and told you what people said.

1 Tina is thinking about doing a comedy routine. Sheila said that ____________.
2 Les and Dina are very nervous. She explained that ____________.
3 Maya has performed in Europe. She mentioned that ____________.
4 Greg has been practicing his routine nonstop. She stated that ____________.
5 Sebastian performed a modern dance. She told me that ____________.
6 Ken and Suzie will compete as a couple. She mentioned that ____________.
7 Antonia wants to make her parents proud. She said that ____________.
8 Greg and Maya will tie for the win. She predicted that ____________.

UNIT 10 — reported speech: questions

Function

As in reporting sentences, when reporting questions the tense in the reported question often shifts to the past. For reported questions, include the *wh-* question word for information questions and add *if* or *whether* for *yes/no* questions. The information after the *wh-* word or *if/whether* follows the word order of a statement, not a question. Note that the pronouns often need to change in reported questions.

Form

Direct information questions	**Reported questions**
She asked me, "When did you graduate?"	She asked me when I had graduated.
He asked her, "What have you recorded?"	He asked her what she had recorded.
Direct *yes/no* questions	**Reported questions**
He asked me, "Do you have any advice?"	He asked me if/whether I had any advice.
She asked us, "Will you ever retire?"	She asked us if/whether we would ever retire.

A Rewrite the direct questions as reported questions. Be sure to change the pronouns if needed.

1 Sarah asked him, "What did you enjoy most?"
Sarah asked him ______________________________.

2 Kevin asked Wendy, "Did you watch the competition?"
Kevin asked her ______________________________.

3 Jesse asked Mia, "Have you ever sung live before?"
Jesse asked her ______________________________.

4 Anita asked Antonio, "How long have you had a band?"
Anita asked him ______________________________.

5 We asked Lila, "Will you do magic tricks?"
We asked her ______________________________.

6 Sam asked me, "Do you have much experience?"
Sam asked me ______________________________.

7 I asked Jeff, "How many instruments do you play?"
I asked him ______________________________.

8 Pete asked Nina, "Who is your greatest inspiration?"
Peter asked her ______________________________.

UNIT 11 — causatives with *have, get,* and *make*

Function

We use causative verbs such as *have*, *get*, and *make* to talk about things that someone else does for us or for another person. This includes paying, asking, or persuading the person to do it.

Form

Form and Use	**Example**
Use *have/get* + (object) + past participle to talk about paying or asking someone to do something for you.	I often have/get my house cleaned when I'm at work.
Use *make* + (person) + base form of the verb when you force or persuade someone to do something.	She makes her children do chores around the house.
Use *have* + (person) + base form of the verb to talk about someone who does a job for you.	We have a mechanic check our car once a month.
Use *get* + (person) + infinitive when you ask, persuade, or pay someone to do something for you.	He usually gets his mother to cut his hair for him.

A Read Kyle's to-do list for the week. Choose the correct option.

1 Get my sister **to drive** / **drove** me to the post office.
2 Have Abigail **look** / **looked** over my English essay.
3 Get someone **to give** / **gave** me feedback on my website.
4 Have my computer **to check** / **checked** for viruses.
5 Get my old watch **fix** / **fixed** at the mall.
6 Have Ben **take** / **took** a new passport picture for me.
7 Make my roommate **clean** / **to clean** his room.
8 Have new software **install** / **installed** on my computer.

B Complete the sentences with the correct form of the words in parentheses.

1 I want to ______________________. (have / my hair / cut) at a beauty salon.
2 Do you know where I can ______________________ (get / my jacket / clean)?
3 Is it expensive to ______________________ (have / someone / shop) for you?
4 My older sister sometimes ______________________ (make / me / do) the housework for her.
5 Mr. Chan usually ______________________ (make / his son / shop) for groceries.
6 It's a good idea to ______________________ (get / your teeth / check) every six months.
7 I like to ______________________ (have / my friends / tell) me if my clothes don't look good on me.
8 You shouldn't ______________________ (get / your little brother / do) your chores.

UNIT 11 — verbs with gerund, infinitive, or both

Function

Some verbs are followed by an infinitive (*to* + base form of verb). Some verbs are followed by a gerund (verb *–ing*). Some verbs are followed by either form.

Form

Use	Examples
Some verbs are followed by infinitives.	She offered to help out at the rescue center. Other verbs: *agree, decide, manage, plan, promise, refuse, volunteer, want*
Some verbs are followed by gerunds.	She enjoys teaching life skills to new immigrants. Other verbs: *avoid, dislike, consider, delay, finish, miss, practice, recommend*
Verbs that describe feelings can be followed by both gerunds and infinitives.	They would love to work on a cruise ship. They would love working on a cruise ship. Other verbs: *dislike, hate, like, prefer*

A Write if the verb is followed by an infinitive (*I*), a gerund (*G*), or both (*B*).

1 consider _____
2 want _____
3 like _____
4 continue _____
5 promise _____
6 recommend _____
7 finish _____
8 agree _____
9 manage _____
10 hate _____
11 prefer _____
12 miss _____

B Complete the sentences with the infinitive or gerund form of the verb in parentheses. If both forms are possible, write both.

1 This website recommends ______________________ (give) donations through charities.
2 I would really like ______________________ (volunteer) with an animal shelter.
3 Have you ever considered ______________________ (donate) money to a zoo?
4 My parents promised ______________________ (take) me out for a celebration dinner after I graduate.
5 His mother avoids ______________________ (use) her credit card for small purchases.
6 Why did you decide ______________________ (become) a financial planner?
7 Maeve continued ______________________ (work) until she was 75 years old.
8 How do you manage ______________________ (save) money on such a small salary?

UNIT 12 — passive voice: other tenses

Function

The passive voice is used to focus on who or what receives an action rather than the agent of the action. It makes writing more impersonal and formal.

Form

Form	Active statements	Passive statements
Simple present passive: subject + *is/are* + past participle	Companies spend billions of dollars on advertising every year.	Billions of dollars are spent on advertising every year.
Present progressive passive: subject + *is/are being* + past participle	Companies are advertising more products through pop-up computer ads.	More products are being advertised through pop-up computer ads.
Simple past passive: subject + *was/were* + past participle	The company developed a new ad.	A new ad was developed by the company.
Present perfect passive: subject + *has/have been* + past participle	People have criticized the ad because of its negative images.	The ad has been criticized because of its negative images.
Past perfect passive: subject + *had been* + past participle	Governments had banned the commercial in over 60 countries.	The commercial had been banned in over 60 countries.

A Choose the correct option.

Got Milk? was a famous US ad campaign. The first Got Milk? ad **1 is / was** shown in 1993. In 2002, that ad **2 was / has been** named one of the best commercials of all time. Since then, it **3 has / had** been featured in books on advertising and case studies. It **4 is / was** being studied by students of marketing to this day. Over the years, many famous celebrities **5 was / were** featured in the campaign. By the time the campaign **6 was / has been** discontinued, it **7 was being / had been** seen by hundreds of millions of people. The campaign **8 has / have** been credited with greatly increasing milk sales.

B Rewrite the active sentences in the passive voice. Do not include the person or thing that performs the action in your sentence.

1 People criticized the company's ads. ______________________
2 They have called the ads offensive. ______________________
3 The company has now discontinued the ads. ______________________
4 The company lost a lot of money. ______________________
5 The company is using different ads now. ______________________

UNIT 12 — comparative and superlative adverbs

Function

We can use comparative and superlative adverbs to describe changes or make comparisons between things.

Form

Form	Adverb	Comparative	Superlative
Adverbs ending in *–ly*	quickly	more quickly (than)	the most quickly
Adverbs with the same form as the adjective	hard	harder (than)	the hardest
	late	later (than)	the latest
	fast	faster (than)	the fastest
Irregular adverb forms	often	more often (than)	the most often
	well	better (than)	the best
	badly	worse (than)	the worst

A Complete the sentences with the comparative form of the adverb in parentheses.

1 I think viewers will remember the new slogan ______________ (easily).
2 Focused online ads appear ______________ (often) than they used to.
3 The magazine ad did ______________ (badly) than the TV ad.
4 The people at our ad company are working ______________ (hard) now that we have more competition.
5 Can you check the text of these ads ______________ (carefully) next time?
6 This ad with child actors tested ______________ (well) than the one with adult actors.
7 This new software will allow you to edit film ______________ (quickly).
8 The focus group results came in much ______________ (late) than we wanted.

B Choose the correct option.

1 Paul drives **the most careless** / **the most carelessly** of anyone in my family.
2 Janet sings **the best** / **the better** of anyone in her choir.
3 Greg gave to charity **the more generous** / **the most generously** of everyone in the office.
4 Celia played soccer **the worse** / **the worst** of all our team.
5 Bradley works **the hardest** / **the most hard** of all the engineers in his company.
6 Of all the managers, Francesca stays **the latest** / **the later** in the office.

Unit 7

Track 2

Host: Welcome to Money Talk. I'm Brad Watson, and our topic today is buyer's remorse. That's the bad feeling you have after you have bought something you may not need. We have a panel of people who have buyers' remorse. I'll start with Caller 1, Steven. Steven, is there anything that you really wish you hadn't bought?

Steven: Oh, yeah. My worst decision was to get a swimming pool. We don't have much time to use the pool, and it's very expensive to take care of it. We really wish we hadn't decided to get a pool. We definitely wasted our money!

Host: I can understand why you might regret that—a lot of people say they regret getting swimming pools or hot tubs. Any other regrets, Steven?

Steven: Well, I work a lot, and I don't have much time to go to the gym, so I bought several expensive pieces of exercise equipment. Guess how often I use them? About once a month! So I spent a lot of money on exercise equipment I almost never use.

Host: Yep, exercise equipment is definitely one of the things people most regret buying. What about you, Monica?

Monica: Well, my husband and I decided to buy a vacation home in Florida. But they can be expensive, and when you have one, you really don't want to spend money going on vacation in other places. It can be boring to always go to the same place, but it's very hard to sell a vacation home. We finally sold it for less than we paid, so we lost a lot of money. We really wish we had never bought that vacation home!

Host: Yes, many people say they wish they hadn't bought vacation homes. Omar, any regrets about things you've bought?

Omar: Just one. I bought an expensive desktop computer, but I don't use it very much because I almost always use my laptop.

Host: That's something that has changed a lot recently. Most people now say they use only a laptop, or even just a tablet. OK. Sarah, what are your regrets?

Sarah: Well, my daughter and I started collecting dolls when she was young, and now we have over a thousand of them. I've spent thousands of dollars on them. She's a teenager now and not really interested in the collection anymore. I really wish I had saved that money instead!

Host: Thanks, Sarah. I should point out that our panel's answers are very similar to answers on questionnaires about things people regret buying. It seems that there are things that most, or at least many, people end up wishing they had not spent money on!

Track 3

lose waste tools useexercise house desktop objects

Track 4

Good afternoon. My talk today is called "Everyone Regrets Something." It is a human characteristic to feel sad about things we wish we had or had not done. Most regrets are about small things that don't make a big difference in our lives: "I wish I hadn't bought this shirt. I really don't like it very much," or "I definitely shouldn't have eaten that big meal! I feel terrible." However, a lot of people also have regrets about at least one or two *big* things in their lives.

OK, so why talk about a sad topic like regrets? Well, if we know what people have regrets about, we can try to avoid those same mistakes in our own lives. There has been quite a lot of research about what older people say they regret in their lives. I'm going to tell you about some of the things that many people say they regret. I think you can probably predict what some of the top regrets are, but others may surprise you!

The first regret is connected to people's professional lives, but it isn't about turning down a job or earning money. It's about time. Most people, especially very successful people, say they wish they had spent less time working and more time with their family and friends.

Another common regret is about friendships. People say they wish they had stayed in touch with old friends. We all get busy and time moves forward. Then sometimes we are afraid to get in touch with someone after a long time. We think they will be angry or hurt. However, they're probably thinking the same thing about you!

The other top regret for many people is, of course, love! Many people say they wish they hadn't broken up with someone they really loved, or they wish they had married someone they loved long ago.

Now, here are some regrets that you probably *didn't* predict. The first is travel. Some people say they should have traveled more. Most people take a lot of short trips and a few big trips in their lives, but how many people really see the world, or even their own countries?

Another regret is about children, but it isn't about having or not having kids. People say that they wish they had taught their children to do more things. This includes practical things, like how to fix problems in your house, and fun things, like how to play a game or sport.

Finally, quite a few people, especially Americans, say that they should have learned another language. Learning a second language can help you with your career, but it's also interesting, and it helps you learn about other cultures.

So, before you make a decision, try to imagine what regrets you might have about it later in life. Don't miss opportunities to make your life better! Thank you.

Track 5

The first regret is connected to people's professional lives, but it isn't about turning down a job or earning money. It's about time. Most people, especially very successful people, say they wish they had spent less time working and more time with their family and friends.

Another common regret is about friendships. People say they wish they had stayed in touch with old friends. We all get busy and time moves forward. Then sometimes we are afraid to get in touch with someone after a long time. We think they will be angry or hurt. However, they're probably thinking the same thing about you!

Another regret is about children, but it isn't about having or not having kids. People say that they wish they had taught their children to do more things. This includes practical things, like how to fix problems in your house, and fun things, like how to play a game or sport.

Unit 8

Track 2

Host: Welcome to *Our Universe*. I'm your host, Sam Maxwell, and my guest today is astronaut Karen Simmons. Karen is going to give us some inside information about what it's like to live in a space capsule. First, Karen, can you tell us how many times you have flown into space?

Karen: Yes, I've been four times. One of those times was to the International Space Station.

Host: Could you explain what life is like in zero gravity?

Karen: Sure. You float, of course, so you have to hold on to something to stay in one place. When you sleep, you use a special sleeping bag, and you tie it to the wall or the floor. If you want to sit down, you have to tie yourself to a chair.

Host: How do you drink water?

Karen: You have to drink water through a tube. If you used a glass, the water would float out of the glass and into the air!

Host: You have very short hair. Is long hair a problem in space?

Karen: Oh, yes. I cut my hair before I went to space for the first time. If I hadn't, it would have floated around my head the whole time!

Host: I had never thought about that! Karen, the purpose of the US space shuttles was to take astronauts to the space station. The last space shuttle trip was in 2011. Do you know if the US will have space shuttles again in the future?

Karen: There probably won't be space shuttles exactly like the old ones, but the government is working with companies like Boeing and SpaceX to create new types of spacecraft that can take astronauts to the space station and possibly other space destinations.

Host: Wow, and do you know where they will go, besides the space station?

Karen: No, I don't, but at some point in the future, maybe even to other planets.

Host: Finally, can you tell us how you felt the first time you saw Earth from outer space?

Karen: It's just incredible. It's a beautiful blue, green, and brown ball. You think about the fact that it's the only planet we have, and that it isn't really very big. You can see the oceans and the continents, but no countries, of course, and that can make you think differently about our world.

Host: Well, that sounds amazing, Karen. Thank you …

Track 3

1 Host	**4** Sleep	**7** Student
2 Guest	**5** Just	**8** Desk
3 Space	**6** School	

Track 4

Host: Welcome to *Science and Society*. Our discussion today is about the effects of space exploration on society. Some people say that it's a waste of money to explore space. My guests today have the opposite opinion of space exploration. They are going to tell us why they believe that the space program is very important to our everyday lives. We have with us Cristina Fares, an engineer; Seth Foreman, a retired astronaut; Lauren Young, a weather scientist; and Mike Bolton, a science teacher. I'll start with Seth. Seth, as an astronaut, can you tell us why you think space exploration is important?

Seth: Yes, of course. Space exploration is not just about finding life on other planets or finding planets that humans could live on. In fact, it's mainly about learning about our own planet. For example, we can study the Earth's atmosphere from space and learn more about climate change. Also, space exploration makes us safer. We have satellites that can track asteroids and predict if and when an asteroid will hit the Earth.

Lauren: That's right. Remember that space exploration is also not just astronauts going into space. Sorry, Seth! Satellites are also part of the space program, and weather satellites give us accurate information about weather conditions like hurricanes and other storms. They also help us predict long-term weather conditions like droughts or very cold winters.

Host: Just to remind our audience, Lauren is a weather scientist and Seth is an astronaut—thank you for your opinions. Now let's hear from Cristina, who is an engineer. Cristina, can you explain how space exploration helps in your field?

Cristina: Yes. I'm an electrical engineer, and a lot of the technology that was developed for the space program has been used in everyday inventions, such as solar panels, laptop computers, and even wireless headsets. How many times a day do you use the camera on your cell phone? Well, the technology for micro-cameras was developed in the 1990s for use on spacecraft.

Host: I didn't know that my wireless headset and my phone camera came from the space program. Thanks, space program! *[SFX: laughter from the audience]* Finally, Mike, you are a science teacher. What does the space program mean to education?

Mike: *[corny and enthusiastic]* The space program is like a giant science teacher. First, it teaches us about the universe, about our own planet, and about the weather. Second, it teaches us about new ways to do things through advanced technology. Finally, I think the space program gives a lot of students a reason to want to study math and science. Space is interesting to them, and some of them will even want to grow up to be astronauts like Seth.

Host: So if space exploration had never started, we might not have developed many of the things we use here on Earth every day, and we might have had more damage from hurricanes and other major weather events over the past several decades. Is that a good summary of what you guys have been saying?

Seth: Yes.

Lauren: That's right.

Cristina: Correct.

Mike: Definitely.

Unit 9

Track 2

OK everyone, so, now I'd like to talk about fake news. This is very much a "hot topic" right now for two reasons. One is because of the large amount of fake news that is out there. The other is we don't recognize it. Although we might be amazingly good at using social media sites, uploading selfies, and texting friends, we aren't so good at figuring out exactly what is fake news and what isn't.

A study of 1,045 adults between the ages of 18 and 34 by the Media Insight Project found that by the age of 18, 88% of young adults received their news from social media. A different study, by Stanford University, of 7,804 students found that 82% of middle-school students couldn't understand the difference between an ad and a real news story. So there is a real need for us to teach young people about fake news.

Track 3

I'd like to talk through some steps you can use to find the real stories among the fake news.

First of all, find out about the source. Look at the website that the story comes from. Then check the text. There might be spelling mistakes, or the text may not be well written. Look at the pictures. Are they clear? If you aren't sure, leave the website and research the organization and its history. Remember that you can trust some websites more than others.

Next, look at the authors. To check if they are authors you can trust, look for proof. What other articles have they written? Who have they written for? If they haven't written anything else for a source you trust, the article could spread fake news.

Check that the article contains links to other news headlines, articles, and authors. Click on the links and check if the sources are real.

Then see if the story you are reading about is shared on any other news websites or channels. If it is, there is a better chance that the story is true. But be careful, because some news websites just copy what others have reported already.

Finally, always question what you read on the internet. Think to yourself, "Some of this story might be true, but it may not show the complete picture." I'll be taking any questions you have in a few moments, so …

Track 4

Male Narrator:		British Narrator:	
1	anchor	1	anchor
2	translator	2	translator
3	editor	3	editor
4	reporter	4	reporter

Track 5

British Narrator:	Male Narrator:	British Narrator:
1 anchor	2 translator	4 reporter
	3 editor	

Track 6

Host: In our special report tonight, we're talking about people working in the world of foreign correspondence. On the phone, I have Dana McDonald, a foreign correspondent based in Mumbai, India. And with me in the studio is Peter Marsden, a translator who travels the world translating from Arabic into English. Dana, can you give us some idea of what a foreign correspondent does?

Dana: Sure. Foreign correspondents write news reports on breaking news stories. Then they send their reports to the news agency that they work for, which is usually abroad. Often we report on what I call "unhappy news"—wars, political troubles, things like that. I wrote about the Mumbai floods in 2017, for example.

Host: It must be hard to do a job like that.

Dana: Well, yes, it can be. But I don't always write about breaking news events. Sometimes I write human-interest stories as well. I love writing about that stuff; I've written reports on a variety of different topics … um, on women getting to vote in villages, for example, and on an Indian professor who is using recycled plastic to make roads.

Host: And what do you like most and least about your job?

Dana: Well, it's definitely a 24-hour-a-day, 7-day-a-week job, which is really stressful. When there's important breaking news, we have to stop whatever we're doing and find out more. But I love that every day is different, and I love India, although I do miss my family and friends back home. I don't see them very often.

Host: Do you speak any Indian languages?

Dana: No, not really. That's why I often have to work with a translator … someone like Peter. I couldn't do the job without a translator.

Host: Yes, Peter. You're a translator from Arabic into English. What's a typical day like for you?

Peter: Well, I don't really have a typical day. One day, I might be working on a written text—perhaps translating a news article into English, for example. And the next day I might be at a United Nations meeting translating for a group of Arab leaders.

Host: And you're a freelance translator. Is that right?

Peter: Yes. That means I work for myself and not for an organization. Working for myself has advantages and disadvantages, but it gives me the ability to choose the work I want to do.

Host: How did you decide you wanted to be a translator?

Peter: I actually studied English and French at college, but then I went to live in Algeria and worked as a teacher for five years. I started learning Arabic, which I love, and then I became a translator.

Host: But you're actually from the US. Is that right?

Peter: Yes, I have a home there, although I don't spend a lot of time there. I travel for about nine months of the year.

Host: Great. Well, thank you to both my guests for their interesting comments. I'll be back at the same time next week with another edition of *Careers Today* and I'll be looking at jobs in …

Unit 10

Track 2

1

Interviewer: Hi there, Noel. How are you doing?

Noel: Hi. I'm OK. A little nervous.

Interviewer: Sure. Don't worry—that's totally normal. Do you need some water?

Noel: No, I'm fine now, thank you.

Interviewer: So, why did you want to audition for the show?

Noel: Um … I didn't. It was my cousin, actually. He said he thought I had a great voice. And, uh … you know, he told me I should try to sing live in front of an audience.

Interviewer: Have you filled out the application form?

Noel: Yes, I have it here.

Interviewer: Great. Good luck!

2

Interviewer: Hello, Caitlyn. How are you?

Caitlyn: Oh, I'm great. Very excited!

Interviewer: Tell me—how long have you been doing your act?

Caitlyn: About two years. Well, I've been telling jokes and making people laugh since I was a kid, but this is the first time I've applied to be in a talent show.

Interviewer: And are you feeling confident?

Caitlyn: Definitely! I'm here to win.

Interviewer: Awesome! Go for it, Caitlyn.

3

Bobby: Hi? Can you hear me?

Interviewer: Hi, yes, we can. Who are you?

Bobby: I'm Bobby Jones. I'm here for the talent show auditions.

Charlie: And I'm Charlie!

Interviewer: Hello, both of you! What are you going to do for us today?

Charlie: We're going to make you laugh, aren't we, Bobby?

Bobby: Yes, Charlie. Hopefully!

Interviewer: Fantastic. Looking forward to your act.

Track 3

Noel:

Well, that wasn't as bad as I thought it would be. I was so nervous—I nearly chickened out! I'd turned up five minutes late and I thought I might miss the audition, but they were a little late starting, so it was fine. The interviewer asked me whether I needed some water at the beginning, but I was all right. And luckily my voice was OK. The big surprise is that they asked me to come back for the first show in three months! I knew I'd sung my best, but it was still a shock. I'm going to call my cousin and let her know.

Caitlyn:

I'm glad that's over! Yeah, um … he asked me how long I'd been doing my act. And he asked me if I was feeling confident. Which I was in the beginning. But then I forgot some of the jokes and I had to make some stuff up. Everything went wrong after that. At one point I thought, "I might as well just give up," but I kept going until the end. There weren't many laughs, to be honest. They said they would let me know in a few weeks. I wish I could try again. Maybe I was just feeling a bit *too* confident …

Bobby:

It was a bit strange at the beginning because I was on stage with these bright lights in my face, and I couldn't see anyone or anything! They asked me who I was. And I thought, "I'm going to let Charlie answer this." He said, "I'm Charlie!" and the guy laughed, which was good. And the guy asked what I was going to do, and I made Charlie answer again. I don't think I did too badly, but I don't think it was great, either. I mean, they turn down people all the time, don't they? I'd be quite surprised to hear that I have a place on the show. But who knows?

Track 4

1

a He filled out the form. b He filled it out.

2

a She turned down the job. b She turned it down.

3

a I gave up dance classes. b I gave them up.

Track 5

Andy: Good morning, and welcome back to *Music Matters*. I'm Andy Harvey. On today's five-minute call-in, we have Elsa Hardman, the owner of the successful independent music company Buster Records.

Elsa: Hi, Andy.

Andy: Elsa, your first job was manager of a record store. How did you go from that to starting your own record company?

Elsa: Well, I guess part of it was being in the right place at the right time. Obviously, I knew quite a lot about music, and by chance, I met a guy at a concert who ran a music website, and we became friends. Both of us had our hearts set on having our own record company, so after about 10 years that's what we managed to do. Buster Records was born!

Andy: Ok, Elsa, let's talk to our first caller on line 2. Hi, is this Lisa?

Lisa: Yes, it is. Hi.

Andy: Hi. And what's your question for Elsa?

Lisa: Hi, Elsa. I wanted to know how I can start my own music company like you. Is it just an impossible dream?

Elsa: No, Lisa, not at all. You have to dream big! My advice is to go out and meet people. Remember that music industry success is not about what you know, but who you know. And remember to ask people with more experience for help if you need it!

Andy: OK, good advice there. Thanks, Lisa. Now on line 1, we have Gabe. What's your question, Gabe?

Gabe: Hi, yes, I'd like to ask Elsa how I can become a singer. I think I have a good voice, but I don't know where to start …

Elsa: Hi, Gabe. Yes, I get asked this question a lot. First of all, you need to think about your goals and remember to keep them small. If you haven't sung in front of an audience before, try to sing at a small local show and make that your goal for the next few months. Then think about the goals for the following few months and work toward those.

Gabe: OK, yes, that's a good idea. I can do that …

Elsa: Also, and this is important: Start thinking of yourself as a business. Be professional at all times. That shows people that you're hungry for success!

Andy: Well, unfortunately, that's all we have time for today, but I'd like to say a big thank you to Elsa …

Unit 11

Track 2

Simon: Welcome to *Money Matters* with me, Simon Bagshaw. Now, we often hear about some of the world's largest donors—people such as Bill and Melinda Gates and George Soros. Their donations make an enormous difference in lives and communities around the world. George Soros, for example, has donated over $18 billion to charity.
But what can ordinary people do to help charities? Many people decide to give cash, but how do you help if you can't afford to donate money? With me in the studio are the local campaign managers for two charities: Pat Beresford, campaign manager for the children's charity Rainbows, and Danny Hamer, campaign manager for the environmental charity Action for Earth. They are the people whose job it is to think of new ways to raise money. Welcome to *Money Matters*, both of you.

Pat: Thank you.

Danny: Thanks.

Simon: Pat, let's start with you first. Let's say I want to help your charity, Rainbows, but I don't have any money to donate. What can I do?

Pat: Well, there are lots and lots of things you can do as an individual, Simon. What we say to people is, if you can't help us with money, you can help us with your time. You can become a volunteer in one of our thrift stores around the country. We love to see young people giving their time in this way.

Simon: But what if you work full-time and you can't do that?

Pat: Well, there are many one-day fundraising events. We organize lots of events throughout the year—bake sales, music events, spelling bees … Some people prefer doing these events because it's a great way to spend time with friends and family. Or, you can make a contribution by getting people to pay you for completing a fun run or a marathon.

Simon: I'm not very sporty! Anything else, Danny?

Danny: Sure. Some people hate doing sports. But have you considered playing games online? Nowadays, there are lots of online quizzes that you can do. For every correct answer, companies will pay a certain amount to a charity.

Simon: Sounds like a great idea.

Danny: Yes, it started about 10 years ago with an organization called Free Rice. Basically, you go online and answer vocabulary questions. For every question you get correct, they donate 10 grains of rice to feed hungry people. It became popular so charities keep using this technique.

Simon: I'll check it out.

Pat: Another thing you might consider doing if you travel abroad often is to donate all the foreign currency that you have left at the end of a trip. Sometimes this happens on airplanes. The crew will offer to collect all your foreign currency and give it to a charity. Last year, we received $21,000 this way.

Simon: Yes, I've done that at the end of a few flights. Well, some great ideas there. Thank you both for giving me an idea of the small ways we can all contribute and make a big difference. *[fade out begins here]* Next week, we'll be discussing what to do if …

Track 3

change
cash machine

Track 4

1 Do you have any change?
2 I'm going to use the cash machine.

Track 5

Interviewer: So, as a follow-up to last week's program about how to make your money go further, we thought we'd ask different people on the street how they manage their money. Here are some of their answers:

Speaker 1: My brother got me into using computer programs like Excel and Google Spreadsheets, actually. He showed me how you can add all the information about what you spend, and it tells you how much money you have remaining until the end of the month. I don't like borrowing money from the bank, so I don't have credit cards, but I use a debit card for most of the stuff I buy. These days, so many payments are contactless, which suits me because I'm always forgetting my PIN.

Speaker 2: I guess I'm part of the generation that controls everything through their smartphone. I use my phone for online banking and that works fine, and I also use my phone to move money between bank accounts and to make payments to people. I have an app that's really useful for my business account—it tells me what I'm spending, but also how much I should pay into my pension and into the business itself. It costs me about $100 a year, but it's worth the money.

Speaker 3: Well, I'm from the older generation, and I think one of the best ways to manage your money is to write down what you spend. That's my first rule. I have a notebook that I carry with me and I make a note of everything I spend and everything I earn. I still use checks, too, although not so many stores accept them anymore. I also have online banking, but personally, I think it's much better if I can have a written record of my money. Oh, and my other rule is to only use my credit card in emergencies. And I always pay all the money I owe every month! I think I'm very sensible in that way.

Speaker 4: I'm actually really bad at managing my money. I don't really splurge on stuff, but I just find money management a really boring thing to do. That's why I'm happy to get someone else to do it for me. I have a financial planner who does all the stuff that I don't like doing. She organizes and pays my bills and checks my bank account—that kind of thing. I used to do it myself, but now that I have a large, growing business, it has become too hard. And to be honest, if I can get someone to do the stuff I don't like doing, it gives me more time to actually make money!

Unit 12

Track 2

Male marketing executive:

When we're thinking about our advertising campaigns, one of the first things we have to do is carefully identify our target market. If we don't know who we're marketing our product to, then it just won't sell. We identify our customers using six different categories: gender—so male or female; age; occupation or job; relationship status—so married, single, divorced, et cetera; geographic location; and behavior.

Once our target customer has been identified, we start to think about how we're going to promote the product, and how to make *our* product the most attractive product to that group of people. One thing that is different between marketing to young adults and marketing to older people is the type of music we use in the ad campaign. Young people want faster, more energetic music, whereas older people—and when I say older, I mean over 60—well, they want music that is calmer and less noisy. And in TV or radio ads directed at older people, the actors usually speak more seriously and less quickly.

Then we have to come up with a slogan. Let's say we're advertising a new face cream. The slogan has to say something about the product in a phrase or short sentence. It has to be clear and easy to remember. We can't just say, "Buy our face cream because it's the best!" or "These running shoes will help you run faster!" We work very hard to get the perfect slogan, but the more often you do it, the easier it gets.

Then, of course, we have to think about designing the logo for the product—and then launching the product in the most exciting way, so people become interested in it quickly. And at the same time, we have to manage the budget so we use the money we have …

Track 3

Ad announcer:

It isn't just about you. It's about your dreams. It's about not giving up. It's about knowing you only get one chance to be the best you can be. Push harder. Run faster. Set your goals higher. Be the best. Because you can. Lion Aid Energy Drinks. The choice of true champions.

Track 4

Speaker 1: Working in advertising means that I spend a lot of time thinking about image and appearance. It's important that we get the right look in our ads. But we try not to over-edit. By that, I mean we want to make sure our models look natural and healthy. And we try to set our ads in real situations. Situations that people can … um … understand and connect with. People in our ads should look the same as the people in our target market and … uh … I think in our latest ad campaign, we've managed to do that. <u>As a result</u>, sales so far have been very good.

Speaker 2: I'm a model, and recently my agent had a photographer take pictures of me for a commercial. They were for possible jobs with a famous fashion company. About three weeks later, my agent emailed me the pictures that the photographer had taken and the photoshopped pictures. I was shocked when I saw them. <u>Although</u> I knew it was me, it didn't look like me at all. They'd made my face look really thin and moved my eyes up and made my nose smaller. I felt quite angry … hmm … Well, I know it happens all the time, but when you see your face changed like that … I mean, do they need to have models anymore or can they just use computer images?

Speaker 3: My friends and I play this game sometimes. We look at … um … magazine ads and try to find the funniest photoshopped images. You might think ad companies would … you know … check the images carefully, especially when they go on the front cover. But there are lots of mistakes. Sometimes you notice things <u>such as</u> … <u>such as</u> an image where the model's leg is missing or the model has an extra finger. Or they've made someone's head look … um … too big for their body. It's so funny! That's why we love ads I guess!

Speaker 4: I don't think people pay that much attention to ads, do they? I never feel like I see an ad and think, "Oh, yes, I really *have to* get one of those" or "I *have to* have that!" It's like … when I'm shopping, what makes me pick up certain things and buy them? Do you think that's <u>due to</u> an ad? I don't think I buy things <u>due to</u> an ad. I think it's because I just want to try … um … *that* cheese or *that* new shampoo. Ads are a waste of time, in my opinion. I buy stuff because I want to, not because I've heard a slogan or seen a logo!

Track 5

Speaker 1: Situations that people can … um … understand and connect with.

Speaker 2: I felt quite angry … hmm …

Speaker 3: You might think ad companies would … you know … check the images carefully …

Speaker 4: It's like … when I'm shopping, what makes me pick up certain things and things and buy them?

Macmillan Education Limited
4 Crinan Street
London N1 9XW

Companies and representatives throughout the world
Speak Your Mind Level 3B Student's Book ISBN 978-1-380-03143-3
Speak Your Mind Level 3B Student's Book + access to Student's App ISBN 978-1-380-03864-7
Speak Your Mind Level 3B Student's Book + access to Student's App and Digital Workbook ISBN 978-1-380-03863-0

Written by Mickey Rogers, Joanne Taylore-Knowles and Steve Taylore-Knowles

The authors have asserted their right to be identified as the authors of this work in accordance with the Copyright, Designs and Patents Act 1988.

First published 2020

Designed by QBS Learning
Illustrated by QBS Learning p. 112; Judit Tondora (Astound) pp. 92, 125.
Cover design by therestless.co.uk
Cover adaptation by Roberto Martínez
Cover photographs by **Getty Images**/Chatuporn Sornlampoo/EyeEm (background); **Shutterstock**/Aaron Amat (lower body), Shutterstock/REALDEE (window), Shutterstock/ShotPrime Studio (upper body-blazer), Shutterstock/szefei (upper body).
Picture research by Fernanda Rocha/Ikonia LLC

Authors' acknowledgements
Mickey, Jo and Steve would like to thank everyone at Macmillan Education and RedNova Learning who have made this project possible and who have gone the extra mile (literally!) to meet up, work together, and throw around a million ideas, some of which even made their way into the books! Jo and Steve would also like to thank Scout for her patience and understanding and for letting her parents get on with it when they needed to!

The publishers would like to thank all the teachers that piloted and reviewed the series.

The authors and publishers would like to thank the following for permission to reproduce their photographs:
Alamy Stock Photo/paul cox p. 74(b), Alamy Stock Photo/Harriet Cummings p. 82(6), Alamy Stock Photo/Tetra Images, LLC p. 114(cr), Alamy Stock Photo/Pictorial Press Ltd p. 68(tl), Alamy Stock Photo/Pixsooz p. 76, Alamy Stock Photo/Alexandra Radu p. 110(1), Alamy Stock Photo/Flo Smith p. 114(tl), Alamy Stock Photo/Stocktrek Images, Inc. p. 68(cl), **Getty Images** p. 95, Getty Images/AFP/ROBIN UTRECHT/Contributor p. 98(?), Getty Images/Ezra Bailey p. 136, Getty Images/ChristopherBernard p. 67, Getty Images/Bettmann/Contributor p. 98(?), Getty Images/Busà Photography p. 70(4), Getty Images/Caiaimage/Sam Edwards p. 102, Getty Images/Vitalij Cerepok/EyeEm p80(cl), Getty Images/DjelicS p. 72, Getty Images/martin-dm p. 70(5), Getty Images/elvira boix photography p. 107, Getty Images/Christian Ender/Contributor p. 6, Getty Images/harpazo_hope p. 94(?), Getty Images/Kauko Helavuo p. 134, Getty Images/Hero Images pp. 85(Martin), 94(cr), Getty Images/Tom Hoenig, Red Chopsticks Images p. 91(b), Getty Images/Gary Hofheimer p. 78(A-br), Shutterstock/Jet Shopping Media p. 96(br), Getty Images/Lucy Lambriex p. 114(tr), Getty Images/Josh Liba p. 118, Getty Images/NoDerog p. 94(br), Getty Images/PeopleImages p. 106, Shutterstock/Richard Peterson p. 101, Getty Images/MediaProduction p. 110(3), Getty Images/Photographer is my life p. 70(2), Getty Images/Popperfoto/Contributor p. 96(cr), Getty Images/shylendrahoode p. 110(5), Getty Images/Douglas Sacha p. 82(2), Getty Images/shaifulzamri p. 94(tr), Getty Images/stevecoleimages p. 70(6), Getty Images/Mark Stevenson/Stocktrek Images p. 78(b-composite), Getty Images/Stocktrek Images p. 78(A-bl), Getty Images/vovashevchuk p. 110(4), Getty Images/warrengoldswain p. 108(tr), Getty Images/Westend61 p, 77, 85(Ari), 128, **PhotoDisc**/Getty Images pp. 80(cr), 86; **Shutterstock**/New Africa p. 110(2), Shutterstock/Africa Studio pp. 82(4), Shutterstock/Alexxndr p. 137, Shutterstock/AnnaElizabeth photography p. 73(tl), Shutterstock/baranq pp. 126, 138, Shutterstock/R.Bordo p. 117(composite), Shutterstock/Bilanol p. 82(5), Shutterstock/Castleski p. 90, Shutterstock/Thomas Cooper p. 78(A-tm), Shutterstock/dotshock p. 85(Asha), Shutterstock/MikeDotta p. 78(A-tr), Shutterstock/Everett Collection p. 100, Shutterstock/Georgejmclittle p. 141, Shutterstock/Herschel Hoffmeyer p. 78(A-bm), Shutterstock/Budimir Jevtic p. 82(1), Shutterstock/AlenKadr p. 131, Shutterstock/Natee Meepian p. 115, Shutterstock/Mega Pixel p. 129, Shutterstock/metamorworks p. 82(3), Shutterstock/Microgen p. 132, Shutterstock/MITstudio p. 120(cm), Shutterstock/MK photograp55 p. 78(b-composite), Shutterstock/Nadino p. 85(Susana, Claudia), Shutterstock/Nika Novak p. 91(d), Shutterstock/Camila Paez p. 73(cl), Shutterstock/pbk-pg p. 70(1), Shutterstock/Pixel-Shot p. 94, Shutterstock/Bob Pool p. 74(cl), Shutterstock/wattana racha p. 135, Shutterstock/Valentina Razumova pp. 122(r, l), Shutterstock/Michael Rosskothen p. 78(A-tl), Shutterstock/Alex Ruhl p. 117(composite), Shutterstock/RyFlip p. 108(br), Shutterstock/Sergey85 p. 120(cr), Shutterstock/Yuri Shevtsov p. 105, Shutterstock/Siberian Photographer p. 127, Shutterstock/SmileStudio p. 133, Shutterstock/spacezerocom p. 91(a), Shutterstock/Vladyslav Starozhylov p. 91(c), Shutterstock/takoburito p. 74(background), Shutterstock/Tortoon p. 125, Shutterstock/u3d p. 84, Shutterstock/Vagengeim p. 97, Shutterstock/vetkit p. 125(background), Shutterstock/Vik Y p. 120(cl), Shutterstock/Micha Weber p. 140, Shutterstock/Gayvoronskaya_Yana p. 116, Shutterstock/Monster Ztudio p. 87, Shutterstock/2p2play p. 92; 123RF/ferli p. 108(tl), 123RF/iriana88w p. 70(3), 123RF/Tyler Olson p. 108(tm).

Additional sources:
p. 98, "Musical Talent is Rooted in the Genes, Study of Twins Suggests" by Jillian Rose Lim, August 11, 2014, *Huffington Post*. p. 98, "Practice May NOT Make Perfect: Innate Talent is What's Required for Greatness in Areas Such as Games or Music" by Emma Innes, May 21, 2013, *Daily Mail* website. p. 98, Gladwell, Malcolm. (2008). *Outliers: The Story of Success*, Little, Brown and Company. p. 104, "Remembering How Reality TV Talent Shows First Got Started" by Bill Lucey, June 14, 2011, *The Morning Delivery* website. p. 116, "Cramming for Exams? Join the Crowd" by Justin Gerwick, June 4, 2014, *The Hawkeye*.

Printed and bound in Argentina

2025 2024 2023 2022 2021
23 22 21 20 19 18 17 16 15 14